Gender and Cultur
the Works of
Indian Subcontine
Select Women Nove

Gender and Culture in the Works of Indian Subcontinent's Select Women Novelists

Lalima Chakraverty

ATLANTIC
PUBLISHERS & DISTRIBUTORS (P) LTD

Published by
ATLANTIC
PUBLISHERS & DISTRIBUTORS (P) LTD
7/22, Ansari Road, Darya Ganj, New Delhi-110002
Phones : +91-11-40775252, 23273880, 23275880, 23280451
Fax : +91-11-23285873
Web : www.atlanticbooks.com
E-mail : orders@atlanticbooks.com

Branch Office
5, Nallathambi Street, Wallajah Road, Chennai-600002
Phones : +91-44-64611085, 32413319
E-mail : chennai@atlanticbooks.com

ISBN 978-81-269-1690-0

Printed in India at Glorious Printers, A-13, D.S.I.D.C.,
Jhilmil Industrial Area, Delhi-110095

Preface

Women's writings in the present world have made a deep impact on the social and cultural ambience. It is perceived as an individual entity, making women's consciousness, experiences and values primary in the act of reading.

Women's literature emerges out to be an outcry of a group of people who have remained suppressed, disregarded and abandoned under patriarchy and vested political groups. The dominant male discourses tied with each other to demote womanhood to subjectivity, neglect, infirmity and structured silence.

Women's writings have outgrown to manifest the knowledge of women's rights, and the collective consciousness of their biological and cultural being. Literatures produced by women exhibit the subjects, motifs and problems exploring their urge for self-definitions at times by flouting the structured norms of propriety as well as abandoning the prescribed norms of gender relations.

Critiquing female writings helps us to view an alignment of attitudes which define the self and the being of female characters therein. This difference of attitudes that is innate in the gender classification is appropriately etched out by the authors who are positioned in their own nation, culture and community. Their ideologies and concepts are irrefutably socially constructed occurrences. This analysis studies women's narrative from a feminist point of view and explores the writers' mind, in reference to the feminist ideologies. But their feminist approach is not applied to undervalue or to nullify these texts in compliance with patriarchy to propagate hegemonic myths and values.

The three subcontinental women novelists, namely Manju Kapur, Bapsi Sidhwa and Taslima Nasrin, are articulating through their novels, a woman's experiences of locations, cultures, language and ethos and their narratives explore these constructs. This book attempts to analyze the works of these three important writers with reference to pre-Independence and post-Independence gender, culture, social and political complexities of their nations. Their work focuses on the area of contention between hegemonic values and the simultaneous changes transmuting women's consciousness, represented as a marginalized section in their own textual narratives. The underlining theme in the textual construction of the three novelists is the Partition holocaust. These writers center on the myriad meanings that Partition manifested for the different communalist discourses, and have highlighted the marginalized status of women within the socio-political framework of the partition process.

In this study I have analysed the women characters as represented in the work of the three novelists—their mental, social, emotional and physical abuse, with reference to the tragedy of Partition and in the political and social extremity observed in the three nations. The work also analyses the reason for gender inequalities and injustices which exist in society. The study focuses on culture and its various ways of assigning different roles, responses, and attributes to the male and female. The novels that have been chosen for study are: *Difficult Daughters*, *A Married Woman* and *Home* by Manju Kapur; *The Crow Eaters*, *Ice-Candy-Man*, *The Pakistani Bride*, *An American Brat* and *Water* by Bapsi Sidhwa and *Lajja* by Taslima Nasrin.

The book is divided into four chapters with a conclusion. The first chapter deals with the emergence of women writers in the three countries of the Indian subcontinent. The chapter has been analysed taking the theoretical framework with reference to K. Lalitha, KumKum Sangari, Rajeshwari Sunder Rajan and a variety of themes presented in women's texts. It studies the female characters presented in the works of the three novelists, as a unique product of writers' imagination, describing the conventional and non-conventional aspects that satisfy the creative need of the artists. Creating the images of women in their respective works, they have created role-models which fulfill an essential urge of the writer to unfold a positive sense of feminine identity. The work traces the emergence of the first woman writer in each nation with the study of the important writers of the three nations till the present time. An attempt has also been made to study the themes and subjects, the writers have chosen for their novels with reference to the socio-cultural context of the countries. The chapter also highlights the literary career of Manju Kapur, Bapsi Sidhwa and Taslima Nasrin.

The second chapter reflects on the Indian subcontinent Partition and how the three women writers have responded to this human tragedy in their literary works. The focus of the chapter has been to view Partition as an essential trope with its myriad meanings for the three writers. The genre of Partition literature has been discussed in detail. The chapter examines the gendered nature of Partition with an exploration of experiences of women and how their lives were affected during and after Partition. The present study also tries to critically analyze the trope of Partition, placed in a socio-cultural and historical situation and a critique by the women writers to compose the tensions and the outcome of the whole process. An attempt has also been made to present Partition from the point of view of states and how till the present time, the nation has to fight with it. The chapter critically explores the treatment of Partition in Manju Kapur's *Difficult Daughters*, *A Married Woman* and *Home*; Bapsi Sidhwa's *The Crow Eaters*, *Ice-Candy-Man*, *The Pakistani Bride* and *An American Brat*; and Taslima Nasrin's *Lajja*.

The third chapter discusses the important features of feminism with the portrayal of women in literature. The chapter highlights the subjugation of women under patriarchy, womanhood and man-woman relationship in the works of the three novelists. The chapter analyses 'feminism', 'feminist experiences' and their significance in transforming society. It centralizes on women's understanding of sexuality and how it questions the traditional cultural ethos. The study depicts how the women writers have written about the social realities, their call for the emancipation of women and the portrayal of the feminine sensibilities. It comprehends the psyche of female characters, their sexual urges and studies the female characters in pain, anguish, vulnerability, abuse and sufferings. It discusses not only the female psyche but also women's encounter with men and vice versa, providing an in-depth analysis of the female world.

The fourth chapter is a social and cultural study of the three nations in reference to the background that has been depicted in the works of the three novelists. This chapter is a study of the various facets of the community in the Indian subcontinent. This gives me an opportunity to write about the unique ethos—the blend of cultures that has come out of the Indian civilization. This chapter is a comparative study of the communities of India, Pakistan and Bangladesh and how gender and culture manifest in them. The chapter brings to light the position of minority communities that has been pictured by the writers in their novels. It also throws light on the marginalized communities and how do they struggle with marginalization, both from within their community and from outside. The comparative study also brings to light the psyche of the community and focuses on the customs and political arrangements that individualize them. This includes the regional and class differences within the target group. The chapter highlights the dominant customs of each community and how it has affected women of the three nations.

The conclusion is the assimilation and incorporation of the main theory that the work envisages.

The book will be useful for the students of English literature, women's literature and researchers in these fields.

Lalima Chakraverty

Acknowledgements

At the outset I wish to express my deep gratitude to my supervisor Prof Dr. Shanker A. Dutt, who inspired me to work in this area; without his invaluable guidance, patience and encouragement this project would not have been quickened to life, let alone be conceived.

I am indebted to my teacher and colleague Dr. Stuti Prasad for so generously sharing her time. Prof. Siddhi Verma, Dr. Joita Dhar Rakshit have immensely helped me in procuring rare material, which I would never have managed to do on my own. I am thankful to them.

I would like to thank my teachers Dr. Muniba Sami, Sister Mary Jessie, Dr. Rekha Jha and Prof. Zaira Kalim who have helped me in sharpening my literary sensibilities. I would also like to extend my gratitude to Prof. Radhamohan Singh, Head of the Department of English, Patna University and the Department of English for guiding me throughout the completion of the thesis.

I owe a debt of gratitude to Mrs. Bipasha Ganguly for her help and encouragement. I must also thank my friends Anurag and Aslam for their help in preparing the final draft of the thesis.

My family was most supportive. My sisters Chandrima and Bulbuli bore my ups and downs, spent hours discussing things with me and tracked down valuable materials. I can never forget the love and emotional support my parents gave me during the writing of this book. I would also like to thank my husband Sowmik for his unflagging patience, giving me a high-five for every chapter and keeping me going.

Finally my sincere thanks go to the ever helpful staff of Patna University, Sahitya Akademy library and JNU library.

Lalima Chakraverty

Contents

1

Introduction

EMERGENCE OF WOMEN'S WRITINGS IN THE INDIAN SUBCONTINENT

> Woman is the earth, air, sound; woman is the microcosm of the mind, the articulation of space, the knowing in knowledge; the woman is fire, movement, clear and rapid as the mountain stream; the woman is that which seeks against that which is sought. To Mitra she is Varuna, to Indra she is Agni, to Rama she is Sita, to Krishna she is Radha. Woman is the meaning of the word, the breath, touch, acts; woman that reminds man of that which he is and reminds herself through him of that which she is. Woman is kingdom, solitude, time. Woman is growth, the gods, inherence; the woman is death, for it is through woman that one is born; woman rules.
>
> (Rao, 1960: 65)

The post-colonial history of Indian English Fiction has witnessed a wide variety of novelists writing on a milieu of topics ranging from social, political, economic, religious to spiritual themes and subjects. The Indian authors writing in English have uniquely placed the context of India in their literary writings in view of the post-colonial discourses like post-colonial nostalgia and awareness with post-modernist revivalism. Interestingly, women's text have occupied a central position in all literary writings representing a high standard of social and literary theories, attempting to examine not only with technique but also with tabooed subject matters in various forms such as fiction, drama, prose and short stories.

Though India has been a land of old civilization such as Harappa and Mohenjo-daro, the matrilineal culture in south did not offer any records which establishes women's literary strength predating the 6th century BCE. The appearance of the first body of poetry by women in India owes to the advent of Buddhism. The tenets of this religion propagated the principle of equality which permitted women to pen their reflections for the first time. Women were also made a part of religious 'sangas' which incorporated the educational, cultural and social approaches in it.

> I.B. Hornor has shown that least seventy-three verses were written by women in the collection Therigatha. The women were known as Mahapajapati, Gomti, Ambapali, Kshema, among others. Bhakti movement in medieval India again rescued women for self-expression and identity denied to them under the prevailing social conditions.
>
> (Singh, 1998: 30)

With the advent of colonial rule in India, the position of women in society was reformed as she was unshackled from many outworn customs and traditions and was given an access to education. The birth of two movements, i.e. social reform movement and nationalist movement during the nineteenth century had a deep impact on the status of women. Missionaries and social reformers made indomitable efforts to improve the condition of women in India. Mahatma Gandhi, Dwarka Nath Tagore, Kashub Chandra Sen and Raja Ram Mohan Roy were the stalwarts who heralded the movements that liberated Indian women from illiteracy and ignorance. Women's liberation movement also played a vital role to uplift the lowered status of women in society.

In the post-Independence period, the right to property and succession immensely helped to empower Indian women. There were subsequently many movements that were called from the lower and lower middle classes from different parts of India, in which women participated in great numbers and forwarded their demands. Feminist literary critics Susie Tharu and K. Lalita in their text have written,

> The food shortage and the price spiral led to starvation deaths. In drought hit parts of Bihar, and food riots broke out in Kerala and Bengal.... This was the context in which what might be thought of as a totally new generation of political engagement (of which women's movement was an important part) emerged in late sixties and early seventies.
>
> (Tharu and Lalita, 1993: 97)

There have been many Indian women writers who have embellished literatures in regional languages—Bengali, Hindi, Malayalam and many more. In the wake of India's struggle for independence, women's active participation in the Gandhian movement led them to highlight the subjects of self-help, self-control, and 'atmashakti' as demand of patriotism and unarticulating the feminist angle in it. The writings do not highlight the immensity and magnitude of their roles in it. Mahadevi Verma (1907-87), although a freedom fighter, woman's activist and educationist, generally writes memoirs and romantic lyric poetry in Hindi; Sarojini Naidu (1879-1949), the first Indian woman to become the President of the Indian National Congress and a renowned freedom fighter writes as a virtuoso of English metrical forms and uses romantic imagery in her poetry. Tharu and Lalita write

> Sarojini Naidu was called the Nightingale of India as much for the rhyme and modulation of the speeches she made during the Independence movement as for her delicate verse.
>
> (*Ibid.*, 1993: XVI)

Kuntala Kumari Sabat (1901-38) a glittering star of Orissa in the national movement, also an eminent poet and writer, writes devotional poetries and rhyme that reflects on personal experiences such as *Anjali* (Offering) (1937), *Uchvasa* (Surge of Emotions), *Archana* (Worship) (1927) *Odianka Kandana* (a set of sad bridal songs) (1936), etc.

Women's issues are subverted in the larger interest of the nation, but writers like Indira Sahasrabuddh (ca. 1890-?), wrote thought provoking journals like *Manoranjan*, *Navayug* and *Udayan* that hold a mirror to the institution of marriage and relates a husband's house to a prison and a young bride to a prisoner. Geeta Janardan Sane (1907-91), a feminist writer, and Vibhavari Shirurkar (1905-2001) in her work, *Kalyanche* and *Hindolyawar* writes on women's issues like women's right to set up her own household alone, and dowry, that questioned the very spirit of equality promised during the reform movements. Such writings definitely braced up the feminist cause and broadened the feminist subject and concern without enclosing it into the other larger matters and concerns.

While dwelling deep into this context and analyzing the women's literary writing, it is noted in the words of Susie Tharu and K. Lalita,

> We believe that there are powerful alliances feminists of all classes the world can make, and equally powerful alliances feminists can make with other oppressed groups if we accept the challenges held out to us. But since the kind of feminist criticism that naturalizes the experiences and issues of western feminism in this way is so easily co-opted by the academy and so widely circulated among third world scholars (while the more historically aware work done by feminist scholars is marginalized), we must explain in more detail why we find the subsuming of a critical method into a celebration of female nature so disturbing. We must explore why it is that if we simply apply the theories of women's writing that have been developed over the last decade or so to women's writing in India, will merely reproduce its confusion, but compound them.
>
> (*Ibid.*, 1993: 31)

Here Tharu and Lalita have emphatically stressed on the unrelated and dissimilar problems of Indian women from those of the West and therefore the stress is not to absorb, dictate or practice what is foreign to our culture and nature.

In considering the women's literary history, Tharu and Lalita have remarked,

> We believe that a feminist literary history must map the play of forces in the imaginative worlds in which women wrote, and read their literary initiatives not as an endless repetition of present day rebellions or dreams of triumph, but as different attempts to engage with the force and the conflict of the multiple cross-cutting determinations of those worlds.
>
> (*Ibid.*, 1993: 26)

The hypothesis they have arrived, discusses that the subordination and suppression of women at the cost of men who enjoyed at all levels should not be the ultimate theme in feminine literary theory. Tharu and Lalita have outlined three motifs: caste and communalism that played an important part in the nationalist movement; subject of gender and class that appeared with Progressive Writers' Association and the arrival of liberal electoralism that structured the women's movement during the 1920s and 1930s. These themes created the framework for women's writing in reference to gender, politics, language and culture.

> Swadeshi (of-one's own-country) movement (1905-08) played a definitive role in the shaping of a national culture. (p. 71)
>
> From about the mid-thirties onwards Progressive Writers' Association (PWAs), which were groups of writers with socialist sympathies, were formed all over the country. The literature, drama, painting, film, music, and even dance of every region bear the impress of their ideas.
>
> (*Ibid.*, 1993: 79)

Fiction has been viewed as the mainstay of Indian English Literature; nevertheless, poetry established its ground before fiction made its pre-eminence in 1930s. This was the period that witnessed the rise of the 'big three' of Indian English Literature, namely

> Mulk Raj Anand (1905-2004), Raja Rao (1908-2006) and R.K. Narayan. Since then there has been a regular outflow of Indian English fiction. The main areas of study of the earlier fiction were sociological, nationalistic and at times philosophical. They have portrayed in their novels their concerns to build a free secular India, independent from the old superstitions and exploitations and also free from Colonial power and dominance. Even the major Indian Women Novelists like Kamla Markandaya and Nayantara Sahgal who came into eminence during the 1950s were inspired by the subject of the independence of India. So we can divide the Indian English Fiction in two categories—male text and female text.

Women's writing in English was initiated in the middle of the 19th century in India with the introduction of English in the 'antahpuras'. Dwarka Nath Tagore (1817-1905), the founder of the Brahmo Religion, was the first Indian, who started to teach English to women in the Indian household and with it began a whole range of women's writing in English in India in the form of stories, poems and novels. The changes that flowed in with the socio-cultural reformation and the multitudinal contour of delineating women's image, performance and position became a significant aspect of the 19th century social movements. So the transformation and the transition that seeped in at the background of the anti-British national movement strengthened the relationship between the nation and the novel in the case of women's writings in India. Since the pre-Independence days, the state, the culture and the patriarchal society have considered women not at par with men. Thus, she was politically and socially considered not as an individual but as a commodity. As has been written by Rajeshwari Sunder Rajan,

> It is also why the most frequent explanation offered by feminists analysts that the prevalence of sati is an index of the 'devaluation' of women, like bride-burning and female infanticide, is also off the mark. In the glorification of sati the facts of pain and death have to

> be granted, since it is their transcendence, or at the very least endurance, by the women becomes the signifier of value.
>
> (Rajan, 1999: 21)

So the women writers when they took up their pens, they wanted to give vent to their own feelings and experiences of life, building a world of their own. This inspired them and they became the first autobiographers in the regional language of India like Bangla and Marathi. The writings of Jyotirmayee Devi, Nirupma Devi, Giriballa Devi to some extent proved to be extended autobiographies.

Since ages, women have been producing rich oral tradition in the form of folk ballads, fairy tales, proverbs and idioms which have harvested a different set of vocabulary and phraseology. Hence, woman writers' works resulted in a deviation from the conventional literary language. The social positioning of woman and her exploration of her own existence accorded an entire range of experiences announcing a different mode of expression. Inadvertently (in lesser terms), feminism was posing a challenge for patriarchy. Their appearance on the literary platform made them examine the terms and conditions that construed their entity.

According to Simone de Beauvoir (1908-86),

> Much more interesting are the insurgent females who have challenged this unjust society; a literature of protest can engender sincere and powerful society.
>
> (Beauvoir, 1997: 718)

It would be unjust to say that a woman writer can more clearly unearth a woman's world, because a good writer always coalesce a man's comprehensiveness and a woman's sensitivity. Still certain differences are quite apparent. The women novelists intently study society's approach towards their own sex. There is an inclination among them to look at the worst of women's experiences. They are introspective about the social norms and put emphasis on the fact that women's predicament calls for a change.

The pre- and post-Independence periods have been portraying the Indian woman and Indian society. But there has been major change in the representation of the themes and topics by the women writers of different generations.

The history of Indian women novelist in English begins with Toru Dutt (1856-77) the first Indian poet to write in English. Her novel *Bianca or the Young Spanish Maiden* (1878) (thought to be the first novel in English by an Indian woman writer) is about a sensitive young maiden whose lover lord Moore, an English gentleman, goes to war and never returns. The touchy depiction of circumstances is scripted in a language that comes near to poetry.

Her books picture the traditional figure of Indian woman of 'Sita' and 'Savitri'. She creates women in self-sacrificing and in confined lives which make them a subject psychological study.

Tharu and Lalita, praising Dutt's contribution in Indian English Literature, write,

> ...the celebrated Indo-Anglian poet Toru Dutt...was a nationalist and a passionate republican; that she was widely read in the history and literature of the French Revolution; or that she had translated speeches made in the French Chamber of Deputies around the time of the Revolution for the Indian nationalist journals.
>
> (Tharu and Lalita, 1993: xvi)

Her novel *Le Journal de Mademoiselle d' Arvers* (1879) (thought to be the first novel in French by an Indian writer) makes her unparallel in the genre of women writers of India.

Tarabai Shinde is the first modern Indian feminist and much known for her published work *Stri Purush Tulna*, first published in Marathi in 1882. The work provides an analysis of class and caste inequality and Shinde offers the finding of women being similarly oppressed everywhere. Tharu and Lalita write,

> *Stri Purush Tulna* is probably the first full-fledged and extant feminist argument after the poetry of Bhakti period. ...Tarabai Shinde, apparently working in

> isolation, was able to broaden the scope of the analysis to include the ideological fabric of patriarchal society. Women everywhere, she implies, are similarly oppressed.
>
> (*Ibid.*, 222)

Krupabai Sathinathan (1862-94), is another eminent figure in the realm of Indian novels. Her two stories, *Kamla: The Story of Hindu Life* (1894) and *Saguna: A Story of Christian Life* (1895), project women characters who carved ways for social change.

Cornelia Sorabji, the first Indian woman barrister deals in her novels the various moods and vestures of women bound within purdha and struggling against the male-dominated society. Her novels, *India Calling* (1935) and *India Recalled* (1936), deal with the above theme.

Roquia Sakhawat Hussain (1880-1932) is believed to be the first Muslim feminist of Bengal. She is a notable writer and social activist of the early 20th century. She is acclaimed to voice her opinion for gender equality and other burning social issues, searing Bengal at that period of time. She is remembered for her rewarding contribution to free women from their subjugation to societal evils.

Sultana's Dream (1905) is a representative work by Rokeya in the genre of Bengali science fiction and is one of the finest examples of feminist science fiction. It presents a feminist utopian world which is completely administered by women and men are isolated, in a living image of the traditional use of purdah. *Oborodhbashni Motichur Paddorag* are her other distinguished works.

The Indian women writers of the early 20th century writing novels in English articulate the traditional vision of women in her stereotype role, showing women in suffering and self-sacrificing roles bounded within rigid patriarchal set-up but being enlightened by the social changes brought in by the rising class of educated women.

After the Second World War, the history of the Indian women novelists got a new vision and perceptivity. From the social and political issues and concerns, the shift was to reflect the interiority of women's being and consciousness. This transfer of interest and subject owes to the contention between tradition and modernity as Indian society encountered a rapid phase of modernization. As women pursued higher education and entered new profession in a big way, they began to explore the distinctiveness of women and the distinctiveness within each woman, rather than beholding the subject of women to one ideal.

In this period, Kamala Markandaya (1924-2004), Ruth Prawer Jhabvala (born on May 7, 1927) are the most distinguished one. Then comes Nayantara Sahgal (born on 10 May 1927), and Anita Desai (born on June 24, 1937) who herald a new era in the domain of psychological portrayal of women characters. Shashi Deshpande (born in 1938), Manju Kapur, Bharti Mukherjee (born on July 27, 1940), Arundhati Roy (born on November 24, 1961), Rama Mehta (1923-78), Jhumpa Lahiri (born on 11 July 1967) are the other celebrated women novelists who have made an indelible mark in the field of English fiction. All these novelists give the picture of Indian woman and also depict the changes that have influenced the Indian woman's status and are responsible for effecting a change in their attitude, their evolution from their victim status. Their novels reason out the family structure and the cast-system (the imperative of the patriarchal social organization). Tharu and Lalitha undertake to present the themes underlining the portrayal of women in the present time as,

> Women's experiences were used as a resource for critical discussion, making it possible for women to share dimensions of their lives they had earlier kept secrets or felt too insecure to confront or even recognize. Groups encouraged women to focus on and articulate anger and dissatisfaction, and evolved through new interpretations of their experiences that questioned and rejected earlier modes of processing and making sense of what they had observed or felt.
>
> (*Ibid.*, 33)

Kamala Markandaya (1924-2004), an Indian by birth was married to an English man and settled in Britain, though she identified herself an Indian expatriate long afterwards. She deals in her novels with the socio-economic factors influencing the Indian women. Her women characters project that the economic difficulties are mostly accountable for their doomed passivity.

Markandaya's classic novel *Nectar in a Sieve (1954)* depicts the suffering of a poor rustic woman, Rukmani, who stoically braves the heavy odds to survive and also like a faithful wife endures her husband's infidelity and penury. She is unable to meet the basic needs of her family which also reveal the poor socio-economic order in India. In *Some Inner Fury* (1955), she depicts three main characters—Mira, the narrator, Roshan, the fire-band freedom fighter and Premala, the suffering wife who sublimates her sorrow in social work. In this novel, she presents the sufferings of these three rich educated women whose agony stem from the uncertain political situations. Though they enjoy all the material comforts, they fail to attain self-fulfillment. Thus, Markandaya in her novels have realistically sketched the image of Indian woman and the finest specimen of ideal wifehood is drawn through the portrait of Premala in *Some Inner Fury*. Her other novels like *A Handful of Ricc* (1966), *Possession* (1963), *Two Virgins* (1973), *The Golden Honeycomb* (1977), and *Pleasure City* (1982) impart her deep involvement with the changing social and political scene of India. She brilliantly portrays the workings of the inner recesses of the minds of her protagonists, their individual conundrum and unfolds their being and consciousness.

Ruth Prawer Jhabvala is a renowned novelist and a short-story writer, who won the Booker Prize for her novel *Heat and Dust* (1975) and also won the Academy Award twice for the best adapted screenplay for *A Room with a View* (1985) and for *Howards End* (1992). Women characters occupy a central position in her novels and she treats them in a comic and ironic light. In all her novels, she has presented the most dismal side of Indian society and family. She observes the social realities minutely and touches upon some of the real and day-to-day problems confronted by the high conventional world.

In her novels, *To Whom She Will* (1955), and *The Nature of Passion* (1956), she pictures the traditional Indian girl who prefers arranged marriage and is contented in her dilemma. They perceive marriage as their destiny and seek satisfaction in domesticity. The novels exhibit the conventional Indian society and the quintessential Indian women's sentiments and approach through the characters of Amrita, Nimmi and Usha. In her novel *Esmond in India* (1957), the character Gulab is infatuated with Esmond. She marries him against his parents, will, though after marrying, she compromises with Esmond and endures all taunts, insolence and infidelity of her husband. But again with sudden strength of will, she revolts against her husband and abandons him. Jhabvala female characters' urge for self-expression and individual fulfillment leads them to examine the norms of society and defy traditions. Their protests may not conclude their problems but certainly endow them with inner enrichment and sense of satisfaction. Thus, the writer with an assortment of characters reveals the oppression inflicted on women in society but they also assume the central point of communion between the novelist's consciousness and the outside world.

We find the Indian women search for identity and justice, find expression in Nayantara Sahgal's works. She represents characters belonging to the Indian elite class and their answers to the problems engendered by political changes. She finely expresses the intensity of the struggle that the Indian women bear to seek self-fulfillment. Sahgal's first novel *A Time to be Happy* (1958) reveals the protagonist quest to establish her identity. Maya is seen to be caged within the confines of marriage. Her silence evokes from the lack of communication with her husband and she establishes the need for meaningful expression for the success of marriage. The novel also articulates the author's affinity with the political leaders like Gandhi and Nehru who illustrates the moral and political ideologies of the time. Marital disharmony occupies the central theme in Sahgal's novels and she describes the mental set-up of discontented wives of upper class circles. She documents the pain and trauma of women who suffer as a result of hypersensitivity, boredom and illness intrinsic in marital life. In *This Time of Morning* (1965), Rashmi cannot get along with her husband and they fail to define 'togetherness', a bond that justifies marriage. *Storm in Chandigarh* (1969) and *The Day in Shadow* (1971) treat Indian women as a self-conscious individual who casts off and challenges the orthodox values and old established conventions of society.

> Behind the façade of Romanticism, sentiment and tradition, what was marriage after all, but two people brought together after cold-blooded bargaining to meet, mate and reproduce so that generation might continue?
>
> (Deshpande, 1983: 3)

The above lines from the novel *Roots and Shadows* (1996) give a realistic portrayal of women's oppression and present Shashi Deshpande's (born in 1938) radical outlook on the institution of marriage. With Deshpande, the works of Namita Gokhale (born in 1956) and Dina Mehta (born in 1945) give rise to a new phase of feminist writing in India.

Shashi Deshpande tries to fathom a woman's relationship with her husband in its sexual and psychological realm. Her novels are an exploration of a woman's quest for self and try to comprehend the mysteries of life. *Roots and Shadows* and *The Dark Holds No Terror* (1980) are such works that define women's self-quest and establish them as autonomous beings free from the confinement imposed on them by society and also liberated from their own fears and guilt. In *That Long Silence* (1989), the author uses the myth of Sita to express the protagonist Jaya's predicament. So we find the writer re-interpreting mythology by adopting new symbols and subverting the classical versions.

In her essay *The Story of Draupdi's Disrobing: Meaning for Our Times*, Rajeshwari Sunder Rajan relates the story of Draupdi in Hindu mythology and its implication in present-day India. She writes,

> Draupadi can be recuperated for feminism not by essentialising her predicament as a "woman's issue", but by remaining alert to the sexual vulnerability and political subordination of women within the larger network of intersection of power and ideology at the multiple levels of caste, race and class.
>
> (Rajan, 1999: 337)

Anita Desai (born on June 24, 1937) gives voice to the feminine sensibility that began to emerge after the World War II. In an interview with Yashodhara Dalmia, she says,

> I don't wish to pronounce any dogma. One's preoccupation can only be perpetual search—for meaning, for value, for dare I say it—truth. I think of the world as an ice-berg—the one-tenth visible above the surface of the water in what we call reality, but the nine-tenths they are submerged make-up truth, and that is what one is trying to explore. Writing is an effort to discover and then to underline, and finally to convey the true significance of the things. If one is occupied in this way, one will be led to evolve some kind of moral philosophy, however nebulous and ambiguous.
>
> (Dalmia, 1979: 13)

Desai is a novelist whose captivation with the women's inner world, their sensibility and struggle for selfhood bring her closer to the exploration of the existential predicament of women as an individual. Her novels articulately convey the innermost yearning of Indian women to resurrect her lost self and claim for self-emancipation and self-dignity. Desai's women characters in *Cry, The Peacock* (1963), *Voices in the City* (1965), *Where Shall We Go This Summer* (1975), *Fire on the Mountain* (1975) and *Bye Bye Black Bird* (1971) are exploring the meaning of their lives as they consistently face defeat in their social and personal relationships. Desai in her writings attempts to examine the working of the human mind and the complexity of human relationships. The novelist observes that the Indian women writers reveal themselves explicitly in poetry rather than in prose. So when these novelists write novels they "are all strangely alike and insipid". She says:

> Women writers write novels mostly with their first-hand knowledge of the basic experiences of life-childbirth, marriage, illness and death and with their necessary close observation of neighbourhood. But something is missing in their writings, i.e., the shaping imagination, that seizes upon the raw-material of life, shapes it into irony, satire, comedy, tragedy or poetry and gives it artistic life.
>
> (Desai, 1970:43)

In reference to her own writings, Desai interprets reality in terms of art and in relation to the artist.

The fiction of the first generation immigrants like Bharti Mukherjee (born on July 27, 1940) or a second generation expatriate like Jhumpa Lahiri (born 11 July, 1967) keep commuting between two cultures. The principal theme in their writings is the dilemma of belongingness with social and cultural alienation, isolation and adjustment, though the approach varies. Alienational experiences and loneliness predominate as a part of the immigrant experience.

Bharti Mukhejee through her diversified experiences has arrested the pressure and strain in the lives of geographically dislocated individuals as they struggle with their lost identities. Her two novels

> *The Tiger's Daughter* (1972) and *Wife* (1975) explore the psychological anguish and societal conflicts encountered by displaced Indian women.

Jhumpa Lahiri born in England and later migrated to United States of America also discusses about the injured consciousness and seclusion of immigrants who try to make their abode in a different land. Her debut novel *The Namesake* (2003) presents the hardships and struggle in the life of an immigrant Indian couple Ashok Ganguli and his wife Ashima. Both these writers have dealt with the themes of diasporic dislocation, alienation resulting in loss of identity, and the cultural clash experienced between generations.

In the Indian English literary firmament, Arundhati Roy won the Booker Prize in 1997 for her novel *The God of Small Things*. It is a story that narrates the tragic happenings of a small town in Kerala. The book presents the catastrophic story of an illicit affair between a high-caste Syrian Christian woman and a paravan carpenter Velatha.

What has been remarkable of writers like Arundhati Roy and Manju Kapur is that their novels are rooted in specific regions and they are portraying that experience with relative honesty.

Manju Kapur comes in the league with the other women writers from India like Kamala Markandaya, Anita Desai, Shashi Deshpande, Arundhati Roy and many more who have laid the base in the branch of female study in Indian literature in English.

As a novelist, Manju Kapur takes part in exploring the feminine consciousness and the predicament of the women characters that eventually progress towards an awakened conscience. Her women characters delve in self-introspection which finally helps them to discover their own self and establish their identity. Her novels *Difficult Daughters* (1998), *Married Woman* (2002) and *Home* (2006) are an effort by the novelist to comprehend the complexity of life, various histories and structures and different set of values in relation to the Indian society.

Each of the above-mentioned Indian women writers writing in English has realistically and daringly portrayed the feminist issues with an intense and charged style in the context of the Indian parameter.

> ...they did not know about the actual location (Pakistan) and its boundaries. That is why all the inmates of the asylum who weren't completely insane were thoroughly confused about whether they were in Hindustan or Pakistan. If they were in Hindustan, then were_Pakistan? And if they were in Pakistan, then how was it possible that only a short while ago they had been in Hindustan, when they had not moved from the place at all?
>
> (Manto, 1955:65)

The new nation of Pakistan was etched out from a part of India by the colonial power and Pakistan was born out of this bloodshed, mayhem and trauma experienced on the either side of the divide. As a sovereign state Pakistan is only 47 years old though as a nation it has survived ever since the Muslims began to make their appearance through the north-western passes and decided to settle in this land.

English, Urdu, Panjabi, Sindhi and Pashtu—the literature produced in all these languages after the foundation of Pakistan have been labeled as Pakistani Literature emerging out from the Indian English literary tradition. The five provinces that constituted Pakistan did not hold a single monolithic linguistic structure. But one of the unifying factors of the Pakistani movement was the acceptance of Urdu, as the national language of Pakistan.

Writings in English in Pakistan did not prosper for a number of reasons. Firstly, during partition, the area comprising West Pakistan was relatively less developed in the usage of English as compared to India. So Pakistan did not acquire writing in English as a convention already embedded in the lineage which could have advanced further. Secondly, Urdu was admitted as the single national language by the entire West Pakistan, excluding the Sindh region. The third reason that is attributed to this is writers preferred to express themselves in Urdu, rather than in English. Therefore, Pakistani literature enriched in Urdu and other regional languages, remained deplete in English. For a long time, English language was viewed as an unacceptable heritage of the British colonial rule over the subcontinent. There was also a class opposition against English language. English was, and then a domain of only the elite class as Pakistani society was devoid of a stable and educated middle class, and not much substantial literature was being produced by that class.

Many Pakistani litterateurs were attracted to literature on partition and themes related to it. The writers in English from Pakistan mainly depicted the Muslim consciousness and sensibility in their writings that was neglected before partition. The ideals of liberalism and socialism that infused the Muslim writers, who started writing before the partition of India in 1947, were pulled into the background of Pakistani literature. Khwaza Ahmad Abbas (7 June 1914-1 June 1987) who started writing before the partition portrays the liberal-socialist perspective of the Indian Muslim consciousness in his writings.

Amongst the women writers of Pakistan, the most dominant figure has been Mumtaz Shahnawaz (1912-48) with her novel *The Heart Divided* posthumously published in the year 1959. The novel pictures the events that led to the creation of the two states of India and Pakistan. The novel uniquely posits the concept of Hindu-Muslim unity and attempts to admit the formation of a separate state of Pakistan. The subject of the novel is defined through the story of the changing relationships of a Hindu and Muslim family. The narrative also tries to understand the political design which created the state of Pakistan without any authorial bias.

Next to be mentioned in the literary arena of Pakistan is Zaib-un-Nissa Hamidulla (1921-2000), a pioneer of Pakistani literature and journalism in English. Apart from winning the literary fame, she is acknowledged as Pakistan's first female columnist (in English), editor, publisher and political commenter. Her work *The Young Wife and Other Stories* (1958) won great critical acclamation which led to two previous reprinting, in 1971 and 1987. The book presents at the background the life of the lower-middle class or a working class of itinerant labour. She articulates the themes concerning the relation between marriage and the role of women and also picturing problems of the adulthood.

It has been observed that women's writing of the India subcontinent in the post-colonial period evolves to be an act where writing becomes an agency to express a woman's tortured existence in a repressive patriarchal/racial society which has tried to silence her. The feminine consciousness that is neglected and rejected but performs on the realm of patriarchal discourse has been highlighted in the work of Tehmina Durrani (born in 1953) in *My Feudal Lord* (1991). Tehmina Durrani a major Pakistani English author in her autobiography *My Feudal Lord* (1991) writes about her ostracized marital life with Gulam Mustafa Kher, an important politician in the reign of Zulfikhar Ali Bhutto government. The book essays her marital life, detailing about the inhumanity heaped on her and how the institution of marriage becomes an instrument of exploitation and abuse. The novel speaks a lot about the internal politics of Pakistan as she belonged to a family of politicians and married into a political family.

Her other novels are *A Mirror to the Blind* (1996) and *Blasphemy* (1998). *Blasphemy* became an instant hit and Durrani was acknowledged as a significant writer of the subcontinent. The book portrays the endeavor and struggle of a Muslim woman against all that is in conflict to the tenets of Islam. The book reveals the deceit of Pakistani maulanas and how they manipulate the Pakistani masses in the name of religion. The book also studies the position of women in a Muslim society.

A novelist of note is Bapsi Sidhwa (born in 1938), a Pakistani American writer, who being a Parsi, her work reflects the Parsi ethos with the portrayal of Pakistani sensibility. In a discussion with Urvashi Butalia, Sidhwa says,

> What the Indian write, or what the Hindu write, will tend to reflect the Hindu point of view and their bias. When the British write it, they portray themselves favorably and present their bias. But there has not been enough writing from Pakistan to defend its position with any sophistication. So I felt I needed to write...stating the facts, because this by itself would carry a fairer perspective.
>
> (Sidhwa and Butalia, 2000: 236)

English language fiction in Pakistan gained new heights in the latter part of the 20th century with the contribution of such pioneering figures like Bapsi Sidhwa who is the recipient of Sitara-i-imtiaz; the highest honour conferred to a citizen of Pakistan for his/her contribution in arts. Her novels *The Crow Eaters* (1978), *The Bride* (1983), *The Ice-Candy Man* (1988) and *The American Brat* (1994) establish her significant presence in the history of Pakistani English fiction. Her novels primarily focus on the trauma of the partition and women's perspective to view the tragedy of the communal divide from a Pakistani angle. Her novels delve deep to understand and portray authentically the pain and sufferings of women of the then socio-political atmosphere of the country. The other themes touched by the writer pertain to the issues concerning the identity crisis in colonial India and the catastrophe of the minority communities living in Pakistan.

Uzma Aslam Khan is the next woman novelist to be mentioned who is a Pakistani fiction writer who writes in English and lives in Pakistan unlike many other Pakistani women writer. Her first novel is *The Story of a Noble Rot* (2001). Her second novel *Trespassing* (2004) records the routine life of Pakistan from the gross societal inhumanity, rampant corruption, power-cuts to love and samosas. The book also establishes the commonality of the lives in Pakistan and India over-ruling the reason for its partition taking both the countries as separate entity.

Like the women writers of India, the Pakistani women writer's writings have become an important platform that focus on the gender and class demand of various periods. This has evolved the literary culture that portrays women's experiences, revise their traditional images and rearticulate their roles and functions. The contemporary women writers of Pakistan display the various ambiguities and differences that confound them and they become self-explanatory in manifesting their sensibilities. Writers like Kamila Shamsie (born in 1973) and Feryal Ali Gauhar, are the best examples of it.

Kamila Shamsie's novels *In the City by the Sea* (1998) and *Salt and Saffron* (2000), won her a place on Orange's list of 21 writers of the 21st century. She received the Prime Minister's Award for literature in Pakistan in 1999. Her third novel *Kartography* (2002) analyses the broken relationship between the main characters, set at the background of ethnic violence. *Broken Verses* (2005) is a novel which is based against the tumultuous history of Pakistan since its creation.

Feryal Ali Gauhar's, first novel *The Scent of Wet Earth in August* (2002) is a widely praised work of her. The work comes out to be a combination of her film-making competency, her understanding of mankind and her innate knowledge of animal behavior. The novel is based on her film *Tibbi Galli* and explores the lives of people living in the red-light district of Lahore.

Viewed objectively Indian literature in English has responded spontaneously to the historical changes in their novels, giving an insight into the changing themes of the various periods. Kamala Markandaya, Ruth Prawer Jhabvala, R.K. Narayan, Anita Desai and many other novelists have depicted the socio-political history of the nation like assessing the role of Gandhi and the tragedy of Partition time and again realistically and rationally. Pakistani writings in English have comparatively reflected less on the historical and political events in contrast to Indian literature. For example, there is not much imaginative manifestation of work found that deals elaborately with Jinnah's influence on the Pakistani masses. Novels like Mumtaz Shahnawaz's *The Heart Divided*, Mehr Nigar Masroor's *Shadows of Time* and Bapsi Sidhwa's *The Ice-Candy Man* have been a major response to the fictional interpretation of the historic-political events, describing the facts with literary acumen. In a way Sidhwa has been an important writer who has come out with the Pakistani perspective to the Hindu-Muslim riots and how it has affected the lives of ordinary people. Mehr Nigar Masroor's *Shadows of Time* is also categorized as an important novel which has explored the event of partition on a serious level.

Partition of India, though was a one-time event had led to the creation of new geographical boundaries with new imaginary confinement that set the idea of inclusion and exclusion. Pakistan and Bangladesh have taken birth from their motherland India. It is a fact that geographically Bangladesh belongs to the Indian subcontinent which neither the Hindus nor the Muslims can deny.

The writers of these three countries though have different nationalities, their literary acumen, impression and objectivity have a common root. The partition of Bengal in 1905 was made under the policy of the two-nation theory but was subsequently challenged by the historic language movement of 1952. The strong opposition against the rulers of West Pakistan led to the creation of Bangladesh in 1971. Present Bangladesh when it was in the territory of Pakistan, it was known as East Bengal up to 1956 and after that East Pakistan. The pursuit to impose Urdu language and the attempt to subvert Bengali language and culture led to the birth of new literature which braced the essence to create a synergetic Bengali culture and tradition. The Bengali Muslims sense of belongingness to a particular community moulded their approach towards Bengali culture, which eventually turned out to be literature. *Ekushe February* (1953) is a volume of poems written in the wake of the new literature which instilled hope and determination to fight communalism and vocalize the common man's life. The cultural unity garnered by the Bangladeshis, shunning their religious differences and reveling in the spirit patriotism in the wake of the language movement led to the production of literature that expressed joy, sorrow, pain and love of the Bengalis. The pre- and post-Bangladesh literature has dealt with different themes and it has come out in various forms like from novels to poetry and in various languages. The consistent evolution of Bengali literature is accorded to the patronage of the Muslim rulers of Bengal. During the Medieval period, literature from Bangladesh touched new heights as Muslim rulers became a supporter of this art form. Chandidas (born 1408), Alol and Daulat Kazi (1600-38) were the famous Bangladeshi poets of the period. Nineteenth century saw a new light in the literary arena when Rabindranath Tagore (1861-1941), Kazi Ahdul Wadud, Kazi Nazrul Islam (1899-1976), Bankim Chandra Chattopadhya (1838-1894) and Mir Musharraf Hossain (1847-1912) made a mark in Bengali literature and it was acclaimed throughout the world.

Bangladesh's literature and literary figures have a deep impact not only in their country but have expanded beyond their borders highlighting many issues affecting the nation and realistically portraying manifold subjects concerning mankind.

Bangladesh's women writers made an equal attempt to create an edge for themselves storming the male bastion of writing and initiated a significant phase in Bangladesh's literary history. Women writers have effectively written about their reflections on various themes and subjects exploring the female psyche and exposing the intricacies of the socio-political nature of their land.

The most eminent writer to be mentioned in the genre of women writers of Bangladesh is Sufia Kamal (1911-99) who is a multifaceted personality being an author, poet, social activist and a feminist.

In 1931, she became the first Bengal Muslim female to be the member of Indian Women Federation. *Bashanti* (*Of Spring*) (1926) was her first poetical work with *Sanjher Maya* (*Evening Beautiful*) was her first poetry publication, published in 1938. *Keyar Kanta* published in 1937, was her first collection of short-stories. Her works portray her endeavour to save Bangla language and culture and depicts her struggle against Pakistani rulers.

Shamsun Nahar Iffat Are also known as Iffat Are is recognized as a significant woman writer, social worker and a literary organizer of Bangladesh. In her literary career, she has nine titles to her credit. Her important novels are *Shona Ache Jana Nei* (1997), *Ekaki Ondhokar* (2004) and *Sukh Jokhon Shesh (2004)* written in a lucid language and tells about the ordinary people of Bangladesh.

Jahanara Imam (1929-94), popularly known as Shaheed Janani, was a renowned Bangladeshi writer and political activist. She was fondly remembered for her efforts to bring the guilty of war crimes in the Bangladeshi Liberation War to trial and therefore she is called as the "Mother of Martyrs". She started with her literary career with her wartime diary *Ekatturer Dinguli* (*The Days of Seventy One*) published in the year 1986. The diary proved to be an important document about the War of Liberation and it instilled the faith of the people for their motherland as an independent nation. The book written in a simple language made a deep impact on the lives of the people who had lost their members in the war. Her other works are: *Jiban Mrityu* (1988), *Buker Bhitare Agun* (1990), *Dui Meru* (1990), *Prabasher Dinalipi* (1992) and many more.

Monica Ali (born in 1967) is an expatriate writer of Bangladeshi origin. Her debut novel *Brick Lane* (2003) was shortlisted for the Man Booker Prize for Fiction in 2003. As the title suggests, the novel is about the Bangladeshi community situated at the street named Brick-Lane in the heart of London. The novel discusses the story of a Bangladeshi woman who moves to London, and how her life gets affected by this change.

Taslima Nasreen (born in 1962), a major Bangladeshi writer rose to prominence globally as a brave lone voice protesting against religious fundamentalism and the Islamic strictures on women. The extremists group of Bangladesh has berated her as a woman who has gone against her own religion and nation.

As a feminist, she upholds the mirror to social inequities and gender discrimination in the larger interest of the society and championing the cause of humanity. Nasreen writes,

> I detest fundamentalism and communalism. This was the reason I wrote *Lajja* soon after the demolition of the Babri Masjid in Ayodhya on 6th December, 1992.... It is disgraceful that the Hindus in my country were hunted by the Muslims after the destruction of the Babri Masjid. All of us who love Bangladesh should feel ashamed that such a terrible thing could happen in our beautiful country.... *Lajja* is a document of our collective defeat.
>
> (Nasreen, 1993: IX)

The novel essays the violence and inhumanity inflicted by Muslim fundamentalists on the minority Hindus in

Bangladesh at the backdrop of the demolition of Babri Masjid on December 6, 1992. Her work is distinguished by two important components; her attack on the tenets of Islam that stifle the rights of women, and her feminist philosophy.

Her memoir *Amar Meybela* (2002) was banned by the Bangladeshi government. Her other famous novel is *French Lover* (2002).

The study of the emergence of the women novelists of the three countries highlights their efforts to express their feminine sensibilities in reference to the society and culture they have lived in. Their literary output with a variety of literary characters is their deep study of the social realities and envisages their motif to bring about a change in the perceptivity of the readers. The women writers are candidly writing on the inner most experiences of women and openly critiquing the redundant patriarchal values and exhibiting an uninhibited expression to the feelings and desires of women.

References

Beauvoir, Simone, de: *The Second Sex*. Great Britain; Vintage; 1997.

Deshpande, Shashi: *Roots and Shadows*. Bombay; Sangam Books; 1983.

Manto Saadat, Hasan: *Toba Tek Singh*, translated from Urdu by Frances W. Pritchett, 1955.

Nasrin, Taslima: *Lajja*. Delhi; Penguin Books; 1993.

Rao, Raja: *Serpent and the Rope*. Delhi; Overlook Publisher; 1960.

Rajan Rajeswari, Sundar: *Signposts*. Gender issues in post-Independence India. New Delhi; Kali for Women; 1999.

——: *Real and Imagined Woman, Gender Culture and Post-colonialism*. New Delhi; Kali for Women; 1999.

Singh Charu, Sheel: *Women about Women in Indian Literature in English*. Delhi; Anmol Publications; 1998.

Tharu Susie and Lalita, K.: *Women's Writing in India: 600 B.C. to the Present*, Vols. I and II. Delhi OUP; 1991, 1993.

Interview:

Dalmia, Yashodhara "An Interview with Anita Desai", *The Times of India*, 29 April 1979.

Article:

'Sidhwa Bapsi and Butalia Urvashi: *'Discuss the Partition of India Subcontinent'*; OUP (2000), New Delhi.

Article: Desai Anita:

"*Woman Writers*", Quest no. 65, April-June 1970.

2

Partition Revisited

PERSPECTIVE OF WOMEN WRITERS

> There behind barbed wire, on one side, lay India and behind more barbed wire, on the other side lay Pakistan. In between, on a bit of earth which had no name, lay Toba Tek Singh.
>
> (Manto, 1955: 14)

The partition of the Indian subcontinent into India, Pakistan, and East Pakistan (Bangladesh) marked the end of British colonialism in South Asia. India's first partition of Bengal was first proposed in 1905, and it continued till 1940, until the final separation in 1947. The term 'Partition' implies a clear cartographic making of a new geographic whole that omits the individual and political changes that is in the company with such remap pings.

Urvashi Butalia's view

> Partition: the word itself is so inadequate, a simple division a separation, but surely what happened in 1947 was much more than that.
>
> (Butalia, 1998: 360)

In the most simplified term, Partition can be seen as an outcome of certain historical, political, and social forces and in this context the division of the Indian subcontinent can be viewed as a colossal tragedy, a man-made catastrophe and a cataclysmic political event that led the country's division along religious lines.

India and Pakistan, the two geographical entities, were mere a territorial abstraction for the masses, until they realized its true and practical implication. The Mountbatten's Plan and the Radcliff Award, they were oblivious off, till it unleashed an era of violence and death upon them. The rush to achieve Partition, inevitably led to a disorderly transfer of population which witnessed the most unprecedented bloodshed. The partition of Bengal and Punjab were also on the basis of religious mobilization, which proved to be a great disaster. The partition besides dividing a geographical unit and culture left a feeling of insecurity, uncertainty, displacement and helplessness among the people of all community concerned.

Partition not only inflicted a permanent scar on the social fabric but immensely damaged pluralistic culture which cherished a number of faiths, sects and beliefs. The repercussion of partition is still shaping the societal contours and context of India, Pakistan and Bangladesh creating individual and different experiential reality for them.

> Partition is contended to be such a traumatic event that Literature, Film and Arts is trying to capture and grapple with it. The portrayal of partition differs from individual to individual. The division of the Indian subcontinent for the Indian Nationalist in simple rendition appears to be a logical deduction of British interpretation of Veni, Vidi, Vici "I came, I saw, I conquered". The Pakistani angle to the partition was the creation of "Islamic Republic of Pakistan" which came as a result of their relentless struggle against the Hindus which consequently led to the establishment of their separate identity acknowledged by both the Indian Nationalist Movement and British. For the British, Partition emerged out to be an unavoidable compunction. British Colonist by 1805, came forth as the largest European force in India, and within 50 years, established their hold on the entire subcontinent. The English were strongly opposed and resisted by the South Asians because of cultural disruption. So Partition came to be the only recourse through which they withdrew themselves, unable to

enforce their will on the Indian Empire resulting in the dissolution of the British Indian Empire.

(Bagchi and Dasgupta: 2003:2-21)

In post-colonial literature, Indo-Anglican Partition and post-Partition works have become an important genre for study and research. Over a period of time a number of writings, including the substantial and non-substantial material on Partition is found in reading lists. The growing and steady interest on Partition Literature owes to the emotional and psychological trauma of the past incidents that has left an indelible mark on the conscience of the people. Such was the immensity of the destruction caused by the Partition of the undivided India, that it became a prodigious work for the writers to pen it. Historians believe in statistics. The historical account of partition is generally an official narrative based on facts with its inherent limitations. The 'aggregate' that the historians narrate in their works fail to communicate a fragment of the enormity of the catastrophe. Generally, figures miss to impart the horror experienced by women before putting an end to their lives by committing suicide lest in the fear of being kidnapped by the men of other community. Figures miss to know the mind of the people when they were experiencing the violent upheavals, when a new identity was enforced on them. Figures even fail to entail the separation millions experienced due to the Radcliff line. Therefore, the creative energy led to the fictional exploration, to capture and reflect on the inner turbulence of innocent minds and societal issues that is still afflicting psychological wounds on the consciousness of the people.

The writings on Partition Literature are of two kinds—first there are writers who give an account of India's struggle for independence and with it they discuss the events leading to it, concentrating on the division of the country. The novels based on the above category are *A Bend in the Ganges* (1964) by Manohar Malgonkar; *The Dark Dancer* (1959) by B. Rajan; and *Sunlight on the Broken Column* (1961) by Attia Hosain.

The second type of novels are like *Train to Pakistan* (1956) by Khushwant Singh; *The Rape* (1974) by Raj Gill; and *Azadi*

(1975) by Chaman Nahal focusing on Partition, discussing the incidents just before it, the tragedy caused by it and its aftermath. These narratives picture the Indian outlook on the tragedy, etched by Partition. Mehr Nigar Masroor's *Shadows of Time* (1987); and Mumtaz Shahnawaz's *The Heart Divided* (1957), describe the Pakistani interpretation of the Partition holocaust.

A huge body of literature based on these subjects has been produced in various languages like Bangla, Hindi, English, Punjabi, Pashtu, Sindhi and Urdu. The Indian subcontinent, before its division had never witnessed the massive migration of population and the horror accompanied with it. The twentieth century writers have tried to examine this historical account, making Partition and national independence as a background to study the other political, social and economic issues which are established by these events.

Kum Kum Sangari and Sudesh Vaid observes,

> feminist historiography may be feminist without being, exclusively, women's history.... Feminist historiography rethinks historiography as whole.
>
> (Sudesh and Sangari, 2008:3)

The writings by women authors on Partition portray a feminist perspective of Partition historiography without being unique and restrictive in its approach. Though this category has a few number of women writers, through their significant contribution they display an aura and perceptivity which are intrinsically feminine. Despite inflicting pain, humiliation, indignities on the general population, Partition invoked a traumatic violation of womankind. The violation against womankind entails their forced conversions, genocidal violence, abduction and rapes in large parts of north India, as well as unprecedented displacement of them. Thus, for women, the Partition of the Indian subcontinent was not merely a fragmentation of the land but it meant, severance of their very existence at multiple levels.

Today I am asking Waris Shah to speak from the grave,

> To turn the page of the book of love. Once the daughter of the Punjab wept, and you wrote endlessly.
>
> Today lakhs (1,00,000) of daughter are weeping and they are imploring you Waris Shah.
>
> Get up, you who sympathize with our grief, get up and see your Punjab.
>
> Today there are corpses everywhere, and the Chenab is filled with blood....
>
> (Singh, 2009:42)

The noted Punjabi writer Amrita Pritam (1919-2005) through this heart-rending poem recites the trauma and violence suffered by women during the riot-torn days.

The harrowing experiences that women suffered during the Partition days have gone unrecorded, due to which the main narratives have acquired the patriarchal account of it. In male narratives, women are either portrayed as victims or agencies and seldom efforts have been made to delineate their social, psychological and cultural experiences of it. So to understand and comprehend the feminine experiences in its entirety, it is better to move into the women writings that are better synchronized to bring out the feminine sensibilities.

It is quite expressive and important that all the three women writers: Manju Kapur, Bapsi Sidhwa and Taslima Nasreen, figure Partition as a central and essential trope. Their novels are based and squarely located within the subject of the partition of the subcontinent.

Manju Kapur's *Difficult Daughters* (1998) recipient of the Commonwealth Writer's Prize for the best First Book (Eurasian region), is a portrayal of the three women characters who represent an allegory of the three stages of the Indian freedom movement. Set at backdrop of the turbulent years of the World War II, and the Partition of India in 1947, Manju Kapur truly presents women of three generations. Kasturi is portrayed at the backdrop of the pre-independence period when India's freedom is curbed and controlled by a foreign power. In the same light, Kasturi is pictured in her own subjugated life where her independence is repressed by the forces of patriarchy. At the background of the independence period where India is struggling and revolting against the foreign power, Virmati's character is sketched. Virmati rebels and fights against that society which refuses to acknowledge her unconventionality. The post-independence period is reflected through the portrait of Ida. Ida establishes her independent status as a divorced woman, whose alienation from all the conventions still leaves her unfulfilled and unsatisfied.

> No matter how I might rationalize otherwise, I feel my existence as a single woman reverberate desolately on that platform.
>
> (Kapur, 1998:3)

Thus, the propelling notion remains that, disillusionment faced by these three women in the three stages remains intense and poignant.

In pre-Partition Punjab, the novel focuses on the story of Virmati, a young woman who rebels against the forces of patriarchy and suffer for her transgressions. Historically, the book projects the period when the country is revolting against colonialism at political and cultural ends. Virmati's resistance to the arranged marriage and her independent decision to be the Professor's second wife can be interpreted as her refusal to the colonization of her 'being'. Though her struggle does not contextualize the national politics, it pertains to her individual and personal contentions. But irrespective of this, the impact of the national movement at the historical level cannot be side-lined. The national or any kind of revolutionary movements seek to encompass participation from women and subalterns, including them at the main stream action. This situation is subjected to the younger generation of women in the novel, like Virmati, Shakuntala and Swarna Lata.

> The Inquilab Zindabad was sung.... The song was so moving. The students' flag representing freedom, peace and progress, was unfurled...and it was clear most of the girls identified with it.
>
> (Kapur, 1998:142)

This also draws that the various movements coined during the freedom struggle emphasizes Gandhi's efforts to make women come out from their limited sphere and to align themselves with a mass movement. However, women's role in the anti-colonial nationalist struggle helped them to create their identity through small resistance acts rather than being part of larger forms of liberation movements. The 'New Women' represented by—Virmati, Shakunlata and Swarna Lata—are stimulated by the freedom struggle and they feel gratified in leading their independent lives personified by the nationalist movement.

> Most families look upon the marriage of a daughter as a sacred duty or sacred burden. We are lucky we're living in times when women can do something else. Even in Europe women gain more respect during wartime. And here we have that war, and our satyagraha as well.
>
> (*Ibid.*, 152)

As it has already been discussed above that how the Partition of the Indian subcontinent proved to be the most tragic and cataclysmic of all political events to affect India till present day. Partition can be analyzed as a major setback in the relations between the Hindus and the Muslims, people who had apparently lived together for many generations. Incorporating this aspect of study of Partition narrative, Manju Kapur in *A Married Woman* (2002) weaves her characters' lives against the backdrop of the communal riots of 1980's which India witnessed in the post-independence period. This aggressive Ram Janambhoomi movement resulted in a series of communal riots in various parts of the country in which hundreds of lives were lost, most of whom were Muslims.

> This behemoth turns its head towards the Ram's Janambhoomi. A temple needs to be constructed on the sacred soil of Ram's birthplace, burdened for so many years by a mosque. A date fixed for the event.
>
> (Kapur, 2002:184)

The fracture and the Partition of the nation relives as millions of people are brutally killed in claiming their identity in a land that has been divided on religious grounds. The issues of 'difference' and 'otherness' play a significant role through the contesting Hindu, Muslim claims. The text charts out the conflicting problem of 'difference' and 'otherness' that communalism engenders in the past through partition and in the current body of the nation.

In delineating the character of Astha, the writer explores a woman's potent interests and concern to be a part of a larger social cause. Aijaz proves to be a catalyst for Astha in making her realize her identity and arousing her confidence. Her interest in politics makes her an activist without subsuming or violating her conventional role of being a faithful wife and a dutiful mother.

In giving us a clear picture of the Ram Janambhoomi movement, the writer essays how such religious fundamentalist movement enforces the politics of communalism. The Hindu militants upsurge led to the destruction of a sixteenth century mosque in Ayodhya, igniting the religious sentimentalism of the subsequent religious groups.

> The kar sevaks declare that neither guns or bullets can stop them. They prove this when in defiance of all barriers they climb the mosque, plant a saffron flag on the highest dome and claim it for their own.
>
> (*Ibid.*, 185)

Thus, it proved to be a threat for Muslim identity and a denial of agency to this culture. This also figures out to be a failure of the nation to resist communalism and laying the ground for a particular construction and interpretation of a Muslim identity.

> Give us three places in India, ...where the Muslim Invader built mosques on our sacred sites. If necessary we will bathe these mosques in blood.... If it is mosques the Muslim want, let them go to the many countries where Islam is the official religion, we are not stopping them.
>
> (*Ibid.*)

In the novel, Aijaz loses his life in such a riot which leaves his wife Peepilika lonely and disgruntled. On the other hand for Astha, Aijaz's death leaves her abandoned and at loss against the normal chorus of her life. Symbolically, Aijaz's death suggests a frontal attack on India's secularism.

Manju Kapur's third novel *Home* (2006) begins with aftermath of Partition. The division of the country which resulted in dislocation, displacement and communal fury is taken by Manju Kapur to set her this novel. A part of 'Home' which is created by the female members of the family, whose role entitle them to be an essence of it; the other half of it is built by the male members who act as the provider, protector and procreator of the family. As the book relates the story of a joint family, with Lala Banarasi Lal as the head, he is shown to be the pillar of the house. The aftermath of the Partition makes him shift his home from

> 'Anrkalli, the famous commercial district of Lahore', to a camp in Amritsar, then Delhi, to finally arrive in Karol Bagh.
>
> (Kapur, 2006:5)

The place Karol Bagh has its history which dates back to the pre-Partition time with a large Muslim population until the mass exodus resulted in an influx of refugees from West Punjab and many Muslims who left for Pakistan.

This feeling of homelessness which can be assessed as the most enervating and tortured experience of Partition, does not deter Banwari Lal's spirits and he recreates his new home and

> 'allowed no regret to weigh down at rebuilding' his family's lives.
>
> (*Ibid.*)

So the history and the politics of the spaces can be contrasted and compared here between the old and new patriarchy portraying the hardships of people faced during the communal divide and the after Partition years of normalcy. The old patriarchy that is represented by Banwari Lal catalogues the sufferings faced due to forced migration, an inevitable and hard reality of Partition. Desperate and uprooted he settles with,

> his seven-year-old son, two year daughter, pregnant wife
>
> (*Ibid.*)

in Karol Bagh. The eminent dichotomy is reflected in the contrast between the two divided regions—his displacement from 'Anarkali the famous commercial district of Lahore' to Karol Bagh in Delhi, an area famous for the same profession of traders. The new patriarchy figured by Ajay and Vijay reflects the change in their ideology and approach in dealing with their business. Banwari Lal's efforts in building up his cloth business stand in sharp contrast to Ajay and Vijay's restful and dicey ways to expand his grandfather's business.

> Mused Yashpal that his father would have supervised every little thing, but what was the use of teaching old ways to the young? Wasting money over architects and contractors, going in for show....
>
> (*Ibid.*, 164)

Ice-Candy-Man, was first published in 1988 in London, however, the title was changed to *Cracking India* in 1991. Bapsi Sidhwa employs the genre of Partition novel to picture the Pakistani vision and outlook on Partition. The book portrays a woman's assessment of the extent and depth of individual suffering, loss of human life and displacement caused by Partition. The text posits the centrality of Partition, presenting a number of characters from Hindu, Muslim, Sikh, Christian and Parsi community, underlining it with historical discourse. Thus, it effectuates a manifold perspective on Partition as experienced by all the affected communities.

The novel is divided into thirty-two chapters, with a deep political rendition in dealing with the cataclysmic event of Partition and writing it from a Pakistani perspective.

In *Points of Departure: International Writers on Writing and Politics* (1989) Sidhwa in conversation with David Montenegro says,

> The main motivation grew out of my reading of a good deal of literature on the Partition of India and

> Pakistan.... What has been written has been written by the British and the Indians. Naturally they reflect their bias. And they have, I felt after I'd researched the book been unfair to the Pakistanis. As a human being, one just does not tolerate injustice. I felt whatever little I could do to correct an injustice I would like to do. I have just let facts speak for themselves, and through my research I found out what the facts were.
>
> (Sidhwa, 1989:36)

Thus, Sidhwa attempts with renewed interest to write the Pakistani version of Partition narrative, presenting it as an aberrations, an irrational act that comes as an impediment to secularization and modernization. She has achieved the text's newness and uniqueness, by not documenting it but rather presenting the communal divide not as an event, but as a process where it is treated as an approximation of reality and not the resurrection of reality. The book also comes out with the representations and experiences of 'every day' life and individual memory that had been subsumed and pushed to the margins.

In presenting the important political figures like Mahatma Gandhi, Nehru, Lord Mountbatten and Subhash Chandra Bose, Sidhwa delineates the characters from a Pakistani angle, thus reacting to a number of books and films which have rated them as virtual saints. By upholding Jinnah in a positive light, she has attempted to revive his role in history and politics not making him solely responsible for the communal divide, following its repercussion.

> 'Don't underestimate Jinnah,' says the off-duty sepoy,
> 'He will stick within his rights, no matter whom Nehru
> Feeds! He's a first rate and he knows how to attack the
> British with their own laws!"
>
> (Sidhwa, 1988:131)

In representing the politics of Partition, through the conversation that takes place between Ayah, the Ice-Candy-Man, Imam Din, Sher Singh, the butcher and the masseur, highlight the instability and inconsistency of politicians,

> 'He's a politician, yaar,' says Masseur soothingly. It's his business to suit his tongue to the moment
>
> (*Ibid.*, 142)

and how religion and ethnic identities have been successfully shaped by Indian politicians and British.

> Haven't the Hindus connived with the Angrez to ignore the Muslim league, and support a party that didn't win a single seat in the Punjab?.... They manipulate one or two Muslims against the interests of the larger community.
>
> (*Ibid.*, 92)

The agency denied to the Muslim reflects the failure of the Congress to include Muslims into its cause as a negation of secular nationalism. In an interview with Laurel Graeber for *New York Times* on 6 October, 1991, Sidhwa says

> Gandhi really sowed the seeds of Partition and turned the whole independence struggle into a Hindu movement. It's hard for people in the West, where he is deified, to regard him as a petty manipulative politician.
>
> (*Ibid.*, 11)

This standpoint, however, does not approve of the Two Nation Theory, behind the formation of Pakistan, and she transgresses the notion of creating as urgency devised by Pakistani Muslims.

One of the most significant aspects of the novel is the portrayal of Partition and its denouement. This is explicitly depicted in the novel by Lenny, who turns eight when India as a nation is partitioned as two separate countries of India and Pakistan, following its indescribable consequences. Sidhwa attempts to diagnose this malady through Lenny's perspective where she finds that when the nation is in crisis, all identity is broken down to essentials. The text also posits that how religious differences are intentionally exploited at the time of Partition.

> Gandhi, Jinnah, Nehru, Iqbal, Tara Singh, Mountbatten are names I hear. And I become aware of religious differences. It is sudden. One day everybody is

> themselves—and the next day they are Hindu, Muslim, Sikh, Christian. People shrink, dwindle into symbols....
>
> (*Ibid.*, 93)

The title *Cracking India*, thus unfolds the tormenting inception of new nation states through breaching, infringing and breaking. Thus, the present continuous tense of the word evokes the permanent separation of the two states associated with ever deepening chasms and unfathomable break which continues to fracture new nations long after its creation.

At the human level, Sidhwa cites how Partition slits the social fabric of the nation and gives birth to a pluralistic culture nurturing religious differences.

> Ayah...carried away by a renewed devotional fervor she expends a small fortune in joss-sticks, flowers, and sweets on the gods and goddess in the temples. Imam Din and Yousaf turning into religious zealots,.... Hari and Moti-the-sweeper and his wife Muccho, and their untouchable daughter Papoo, become even more untouchable as they are entrenched deeper in their low Hindu caste.
>
> (*Ibid.*)

It has been marked in the text that Sidhwa does not adhere to the presentation of exact dates in accordance to the historical events. Gandhi's noted salt march to Dandi, which took place in 1930s, is falsely presented during the pre-Partition months of 1947. This occasions the blurring Partition memories of the narrator though with a modified historicist approach. Similarly, Gandhi's visit to Lahore in the early months of 1947 may not be historically accurate, but it gives the author an opportunity to reappraise his role in history. Sidhwa's parody of Gandhi is evident from the comic portrayal of him as narrated by Lenny. She not only mocks at his appearance,

> He is small, dark, shrivelled, old. He looks just like Hari our gardener, except he has a disgruntled, disgusted and irritable look,...
>
> (*Ibid.*, 86)

but also about his beliefs and ideals. Lenny describes Gandhi as

> "an improbable toss-up between a clown and a demon" and end up making such generalizations as
>
> "He is a man who loves women. And lame children.
>
> And the untouchable sweeper—so he will love the untouchable
>
> Sweeper's constipated girl-child best."
>
> (*Ibid.*, 87)

Sidhwa not only makes Gandhi accountable for Partition, but also shows him to be inconsistent and changing alliances according to his requirement. Tarnishing his deified image, Sidhwa through Lenny discredits his belief on 'non-violence', but also charges him for evoking communal tensions.

> It wasn't until some years later—when I realized the full scope and dimension of the massacres—that I comprehended the concealed nature of the ice lurking deep beneath the hypnotic and dynamic feminity of Gandhi's non-violent exterior.
>
> (*Ibid.*, 88)

Sidhwa depicts Akali Dal leader Master Tara Singh, as the Sikh soldier—saint, and presents him as a perpetrator of violence,

> holding a long sword in each hand, the curved steel reflecting the sun's glare as he clashes the sword above his head.
>
> (*Ibid.*, 133)

She is of the opinion that Muslims in East Punjab were victimized because of the violence and terror generated by the Sikhs, who were manipulated by politicians. The narrative of Sikh's attack on the Muslim village of Pir Pindo in Punjab may lack in historical accuracy, but there is evidence of such onslaught that took place when partition was eminent. Thus, Sidhwa keeps the readers informed about the ever shifting political scene through Ayah's admirers, thereby connecting the political with the personal.

Lenny's nightmares becomes suggestive of the violence and terror unleased by the Partition holocaust in which the innocent is engulfed and brutally victimized by the powerful. Howsoever, Lenny being a part of a different community does not affect her directly. The stark dichotomy between two circumstances are portrayed—once where the characters are ordinary people leading normal lives and then

> suddenly Lenny realizes the otherness growing within them, which gives her an insight into the undercurrent that will tear the community apart...because of their religious and political differences.
>
> (*Ibid.*, 186)

Lenny observes overnight the appearance of Lahore being fragmented into religious groups. The trauma of violence at emotional and psychological levels is presented as a series of events and images illustrating human loss and agony. The recoiling of human beings into religious signifiers become evident, when a Sikh assemblage holds a

> naked child, twitching on a spear struck between her shoulders, (waving it) like a flag.
>
> (*Ibid.*, 199)

The vivid imagery, used by Sidhwa to convey the horror and pointless brutality of communal divide is exemplified as

> "the peasants died of sword and spear wounds in the slushy lanes and courtyards" (p. 199); "the old mullah's face was serene in death, his beard pale against the brick plinth" (p. 203); "there are no young women among the dead! Only two gunny-bags full of women's breast!" (p. 149); "They drag Ayah out. They drag her by her arms stretched taut, and her bare feet....
>
> (*Ibid.*, 183)

The poignant and painful aspect of the Partition is etched out when the cartographic division of the earth assigns a separate and distinct identity to an individual overnight. The long enduring feeling of oneness with one's land is brutally slashed and a person is prosecuted with a separate and detached existence altogether.

> "Those Mussulmans who want to go to Pakistan had better get into the truck...." What? the puzzled villagers asked. "Is Pakistan already there?"
>
> (*Ibid.*, 110)

The text registers not only the dislocation and uprootedness of Partition but also essays the plight and predicament of women, as they become the symbol and metaphor of a fixed religious group. The raped and ravished female body becomes the signifier of disgrace and humiliation of one's ethnic, religious and national gendered subject. The sanctity of the female body symbolizes the purity of the nation and therefore raped woman cannot become the conveyer of the unblemished image required for the narration of the nation.

As a symbol Ayah is raped by her Muslim admires and taken to Hira Mandi and married to Ice-Candy-Man. Lenny's Godmother rescues her and helps her to cross the border under police protection. This makes it eminent that the avoidance of rape leaves woman with option of committing suicide, so that she can be placed within the co-text of nation as legitimate and untainted—although being dead. The survivor of rape is denied entry into the lawful territory of the nation. Therefore, Ayah's refusal to stay with Ice-Candy-Man confronts her with such questions as

> What if your family won't take you back? She asks.
>
> (*Ibid.*, 262)

The two 'fallen women'—Ayah and Hamida—are rescued by Lenny's extended family. Lenny's mother and aunt helped the people to migrate by

> smuggling rationed petrol to help (their) Hindu and Sikh friends to run away.... And also for the convoys to send kidnapped women like (Lenny's Ayah) to their families across the border.
>
> (*Ibid.*, 254)

This enables Ayah to leave prostitution and Hamida is restored as the new nanny for Lenny.

The massive killings planned by the various religious dominations registers also the possibility of men evading death by identifying one's body with another community. For example, Hari, the gardener is converted to 'Himmat Ali' by his newly circumcised penis and his talent to recite Kalma with

> the cadence and intonations of Hindu chants.
>
> (*Ibid.*, 181)

But, on the other side, Ayah cannot resort to such bodily transformation and is pulled away by

> harsh hands, supporting her with careless intimacy.
>
> (*Ibid.*, 183)

Thus, the vivisection of the nation occasions the creation of new homelands which becomes the space for indescribable horrors for people who have to switch across the newly created borders in the name of religion, region and ethnic essentialness.

Sidhwa scripts the story of *The Pakistani Bride* (1983) against the backdrop of the 'chaotic summer of 1947' (p. 14).

The Pakistani Bride echoes the author's desire to comprehend the terrible events of the Partition of the Indian subcontinent in 1947.

> hot lands of the Punjab were suddenly ripped into two territories—Hindu and Muslim, India and Pakistan.
>
> (Sidhwa, 1990:14)

The novel emanates with Partition and the devastation that followed it. It also gives an account of the disruption and how people of a nation become the symbolic manifestation of pain, loss and trauma. The book gives a truthful representation of Partition, narrating the violence and brutalization that marked it.

> A Sikh, hair streaming, lashed a bloody sword. Another slowly waved a child stuck at the end of his spear like a banner.
>
> (*Ibid.*, 28)

The tragedy of Partition holocaust depicts Zaitoon, a Punjabi girl being orphaned as a result of the communal tensions that accompanied the formation of India and Pakistan. In depicting the horror and loss of the Partition trauma, Sidhwa shows Zaitoon's parents being killed in such a communal strife. She explores the vulnerability of the people victimized by the tragedy of Partition when their mode of conveyance is attacked by a 'standing mob'.

> Trains carrying refugees sped through the darkness of the night.... They left at odd hours to try to dodge mobs bent on their destruction. Yet trains were ambushed and looted and their fleeing occupants slaughterd.
>
> (*Ibid.*, 15)

The author here has contextualized the magnitude of the dehumanizing act of Partition in giving a real picture of the 'Refugee Special' trains. She describes these trains as virtual death bed for thousands of people who have left their home and hearth to seek security across a line that has neither been sketched nor desired. She projects the trauma and sufferings of the minority communities who are mercilessly victimized during Partition.

The deep seated enmity and hostility intensified during Partition in the form of communal strife, leading to unprecedented violence and rampage serves as 'an agreement' between the warring communities. The individuals become the token of their group and are ruthlessly hunted and ravished in the execution of 'the agreement'.

> The carnage is subsiding.... The dying and the dead are being looted of their bloodied ornaments and weapons. An eerie silence settles on the stench of blood.
>
> (*Ibid.*, 29)

Thus, Zaitoon's parents, Sikander and Johra's death in such a communal strife serves as a microcosm in the Partition violence that is stricken by murder, loot, abduction and widespread devastation. Sidhwa in creating her work in realistic mode of writing, explicitly draws the consequences of forced migration. This forced displacement and dislocation from ancestral home resulted in the abandonment of property for which one has worked so hard and finally endowing them with fractured identities.

> The train at Ludhiana station already swarmed with Muslims who had boarded it at earlier stops. Panic-stricken families were abandoning their animals and possessions in an attempt to get on.
>
> (*Ibid.*, 18)

The novel unfolds a story of a battle of values which applies as a metaphor of a similar conflict between the two religious communities of Hinduism and Islam. Zaitoon is married in a marginalized ethnic group of Kohistan tribe in Pakistan and is unable to fit herself in such a society. She is victimized and treated as a slave by her husband as a standard of honourable behaviour. Such code of behaviour proves to be a reason of unending sorrow for women and an infringement of such a system, a woman had to pay with her life.

> Honour! She thought bitterly. Everything for honour—And another life lost! Her loved ones dead and now the girl she was beginning to hold so dear sacrificed. She knew the infalliability of the mountain huntsmen.
>
> (*Ibid.*, 190)

> The same conflict is witnessed in the colossal tragedy of partition, where a woman is made to suffer and bear the atrocities doubly as she becomes a signifier and token of honour of the religious community and the family to which she belongs. So a woman is raped and sexually assaulted or to escape this trauma she had to opt for self annihilation as women's sexuality occupied an intrinsic place in the enactment of violence during Partition. Assaulting a woman's body became a manifestation of victory of one community over the other.
>
> (Jain, 2007:233-51)

Sidhwa's deep interest to portray the creation of Pakistan as a nation in her novel has been done explicitly in *Ice-Candy-Man* and partially in *The Pakistani Bride*. Her area of interest is not only restricted to this but ranges from the pre-independence to Partition and post-independence socio-political scenario of Pakistan. This justifies her novels being a systematic exploration of the theme of Partition, treating it not as an event but as a process. *The Crow Eaters* and *The Pakistani Bride* describe the background before the Partition of 1947. *Ice-Candy-Man* depicts the Partition violence and *An American Brat* discusses the socio-political scene after Partition.

One of the major subjects handled by Sidhwa in all her subsequent novels is the treatment of the Parsis in the colonial rule and their approach towards the Partition of Indian subcontinent.

The novel *The Crow Eaters* (1980) presents the Parsis's devotion and obedience towards the colonial rule and their contempt for the national movement.

> Things were going smoothly; there has always been throwing off the British yoke—of Independence—but that fool of a Parsi starts smoothing called the Congress....
>
> (Sidhwa, 1980:282)

The writer articulately delineates the character of Fardoon Junglewalla who does not hesitate to refer himself as "the greatest toddies of the British Empire" (p. 12) and identifies himself with the Colonial power. The Parsis adopting a neutral stance and displaying immense practicality veered their loyalty towards the majority when the shadow of Partition dawned upon them.

> Fardoon said softly, "We will stay where we are...let Hindus, Muslims, Sikhs, or whoever, rule. What does it matter? The sun will continue to rise and the sun continue to set...." (*Ibid.*, 283)

Sidhwa traces the advent of the Parsis in the Indian subcontinent as,

> Booted out of Persia at the time of the Arab invasion 1,300 years ago, a handful of our ancestors fled to India with their sacred fires.
>
> (*Ibid.*, 11)

and what has been assessed by the writer here is that though the British never allotted equal status to the Parsis, they enjoyed a favourable position in British India.

> They are our sovereigns! Where do you think we'd be if we did not curry favour? Next to the nawabs, rajas and princelings, we are the greatest toadies of the British empire!
>
> (*Ibid.*, 12)

However, Sir Easy Money emphasizes the global identity of the Parsis rather than the nationalist,

> One leg in India and one leg in England. We are citizens of the world.
>
> (*Ibid.*, 168)

The inability to associate with any of the religious community leaves Freddy's family and friends without a homeland and they relocate from Pakistan to India and vice versa. The divided line demarcating the two boundaries of the nation have been further analysed by Sidhwa in *An American Brat* (1993).

The dilemma of the Parsis in identifying themselves with an alien culture and their undecided approach towards the freedom struggle did not restrict them from participating in it. This motif has been developed by Sidhwa in *An American Brat,* where the Parsi community is shown actively participating in Pakistani politics.

This novel focuses the time after the creation of Pakistan and the Parsis's deep insecurity and fear in a nation, where the fundamentalist Islam usurps an individual's personal space and identity. Zareen Ginwalla feels threatened in such an atmosphere where,

> the zealous Islamization fostered by General Zia, which encouraged religious chauvinism and marginalized people like her—the minorities—and make them vulnerable to petty ill will.
>
> (Sidhwa, 1994:238)

In this novel, we observe Sidhwa not being sympathetic towards the Pakistani leaders and its politics. She presents the post-independence scenario of Pakistan when the army under General Zia-ul-Haq grabbed control of the nation in 1978. Zulfikar Ali Bhutto was tried for corruption and murder and sentenced to death in 1978. The worldwide appeal for clemency was unheard and Pakistan was entirely under the control of fundamentalist politics.

> The length of the letter and the details with which it was packed, gave Feroza a clear idea of the grief Bhutto's hanging had caused Zareen and many other like her in Pakistan.
>
> (*Ibid.*, 183)

Sidhwa through Zareen also protests against the unequal Hadood Ordinance passed by the Pakistani government under which a victim of rape was considered an offender and was penalized.

> The blind sixteen-year-old servant girl, pregnant out of wedlock as a result of rape, was charged with adultery. she was sentenced to three years rigorous imprisonment, fifteen lashes, and a fine of thousand rupees.
>
> (*Ibid.*, 236)

Sidhwa highlights the bigoted and puritanical outlook of the Pakistani politics and how it adversely affected and debased women in Pakistan.

> In Pakistan, politics concerned everyone—from the street sweeper to the business tycoon—because it personally affected everyone, particularly women, determining how they should dress...how they should conduct themselves even within the four walls of their homes.
>
> (*Ibid.*, 171)

Zareen bitterly resents this and sends her daughter to America so that she does not fall a prey to this silent victimization. When the mother and daughter are acquainted with the American ethos and culture, they realize the hypocrisy attached to the Parsi Zorastrian patriarchy. America incites in

Zareen with a progressive outlook which cites the possibility of her permitting Feroza to marry her American boyfriend.

> She had often opined how unfair it was that while a Parsee man who married a "non" could keep his faith and bring up his children as Zorostrians, a Parsee woman could not.... But with Feroza's happiness at stake and her strengthening affection for David, Zareen wondered about it.
>
> (*Ibid.*, 287)

David, however, could not come to terms with the conventions attached to the Parsi Zorastrian life and pulls himself out from Feroza's life. Left alone she seeks solace in her ancient religion

> Feroza dug out her sudra and kusti...she said her kusti prayers and stood, hands joined, invoking Ahura Mazda's blessings and favour.
>
> (*Ibid.*, 317)

Taslima Nasreen is the third woman writer to figure the holocaust of the Partition violence and its consequent communal unrest in her text *Lajja*, which centers around the anti-Hindu riots, which broke out in different parts of Bangladesh after the demolition of Babri Masjid in India on 6 December 1992. The reaction to this demolition lashed out in the form of senseless violence against the Hindus in Bangladesh. Nasreen essays the frightful impact of religious fundamentalism on human race through this novel. This text posits the contemporary debate on communalism at its background and tries to understand the complexity attached to the historically received and accepted identity of Hindus and Muslims in a nation.

> The suffering the victims and their families felt was also the same, no matter what their religion.... Was he afraid, by virtue of being a Hindu, of being an insecure, fearful human in his own home?
>
> (Nasreen, 1993:18)

The severance of the Bengal region into East and West Bengal did not redress the problem of communal tensions as it was cited during the Partition of the Indian subcontinent. The book probes the whole agenda of secularization and modernization and the nation's intrinsic claim to nationalism.

> The state of Bangladesh was founded on the basis of four major Principles: nationalism, secularism, democracy and socialism. The country had worked long and hard for its independence...after independence, the reactionaries who had been against the very spirit of independence had gained power....
>
> (*Ibid.*, 43)

Lajja accounts the story of a Hindu family in Bangladesh; a family which is torn asunder by the oppressive fundamentalist forces. The book outlines the devastation of Dutta family in particular, a family that had to pay the prize for the demolition of Babri Masjid in Ayodhya, a far-off place from Bangladesh. The book apart from presenting this also documents the tribulations and ordeal of a nation curbed by religious fundamentalism.

> Thus, unlawfully and unconstitutionally, Islam became the national religion of Bangladesh. As a result, communalism and religious fanaticism exploded out of control.
>
> (*Ibid.*)

The venom of communalism explodes and takes its toll on Sudhamoy, Kironmoyee, Suranjan and Maya who suffer invariably because of their belonging to a religious minority in a nation which is dominated by Muslim at large. They become the 'unarticulated' other and are seen as the cause of wholesale massacres, becoming the subjects of vengeance. The net result is that the religious majority serves to isolate, marginalize and discriminate its own inhabitants who form the religious minority.

> All over the subcontinent, in the name of religion, riots were rampant. The minorities were brutalized, and Suranjan being a minority himself understood their plight...no Hindu in Bangladesh could be blamed for the troubles visited on Muslims by their Hindu countrymen.

> How could Suranjan drive in this simple logic? Who would listen to him?
>
> (*Ibid.*, 89)

The essential factor underlined by the writer is not the antagonistic relationship shared by the Hindu and Muslim communities but the similarity between the fundamentalists belonging to the two religious communities who are invested with a disruptive power that strikes at the very root of the normalcy of the nation.

> Strangely enough, there is no dispute between Hindu fanatics and Muslim fanatics. You must have noticed the similarities between the Jamaatis in this country and the BJP in India.... One thousand people have died in the riots in India. The Vishwa Hindu Parishad, the RSS, the Bajrang Dal...groups have all been banned".
>
> (*Ibid.*, 111)

The text bespeaks the ferocity and violence of Partition that persists and erupts in such communal riots. The identity that is typified by each individual member attains the process of violence. The violence that is directed at effacing the identity of marginal group either by forcing them to embrace their religion or to leave the country. The determination of Sudhmoy to stick to his motherland is meted out with disastrous consequences. The woe of the Partition violence inflicts its indelible scars on the body and mind of Sudhamoy and he is brutally punished for his Hindu identity and his unacceptance of the other religious faith.

> One day, after Sudhamoy had again thwarted their efforts, they jerked up his lungi, and mutilated his penis.
>
> (*Ibid.*, 66)

His feeling of oneness with his homeland and being a true and sincere lover of humanity, he becomes a victim to the gross inhumanity, particularly sectarian violence. It becomes a crude irony that the family's love for their motherland did not rescue them and they lose their daughter who is kidnapped and presumably raped and killed.

> Maya's hands were still soiled with the rice and curry.... Her clothes were in disarray as wild-eyed she screamed to her mother for help.
>
> (*Ibid.*, 148)

The text ostensibly deals with a nation and society that has lost all human and rational values and have succumbed to religious discrimination. The book stands as a mirror projecting a country which violates the very secular spirit of the Constitution of Bangladesh. Nasreen says,

> There is no Hindu in the administration. Since Pakistani times no Hindu has been appointed to the post of Secretary.
>
> (*Ibid.*, 137)

The writer makes emphatic statements in presenting the politics of Bangladesh, and writes,

> Democracy was clearly not strong enough to arrest the spread of communalism. On the other hand, the communal groups had much more strength and working towards the fulfillment of their goals.
>
> (*Ibid.*, 178)

In exposing the Constitutional framework of Bangladesh Nasreen further writes,

> In 1978, the commencement of the constitution of 1972 was changed to 'Bismiillahir Rahmanir Rahim' and in due course of time the 'Secularism' was removed and clause 25 (2) now read 'The State shall endeavour, preserve and strengthen the fraternal relation among Muslim countries based on Islamic solidarity.
>
> (*Ibid.*, 183)

Thus, the three women writers who belong to the three separate countries of one subcontinent address to the politics of Partition and the politics of communalism which emerges out from it. In putting the Partition holocaust at the backdrop of their novels, they have assessed its impact according to their own respective angle and interpreting how India's past has come to play an ever-important role in the rhetoric of contemporary politics.

References

Batulia, Urvashi: *The Other Side of Silence, Voices from the Partition of India.* New Delhi; Penguin; 1998.

Bagchi Jasodhara, Dasgupta Subhoranjan: *The Trauma and Triumph of Gender and Partition.* New Delhi; Shree Publication; 2003.

Jain, Jasbir: *Reading Partition/Living Partition.* New Delhi; Rawat Publication; 2007.

Kapur, Manju: *Difficult Daughters.* New Delhi; Faber and Faber; 1998.

Kapur, Manju: *A Married Woman.* New Delhi; India Ink (Roli Books); 2002.

Kapur, Manju: *Home.* New Delhi; Random House India; 2006.

Manto, Saadat, Hasan: *Toba Tek Singh*, translated from Urdu by Frances W. Pritchett, 1955.

Nasrin, Taslima: *Lajja.* New Delhi; Penguin Books; 1993.

Sidhwa, Bapsi: "Points of Departure—International Writers on Writing and Politics". 1989.

Sidhwa, Bapsi: *Ice-Candy–Man.* New Delhi; Penguin Books; 1988.

Sidhwa, Bapsi: *The Pakistani Bride.* New Delhi; Penguin Books; 1990.

Sidhwa, Bapsi: *The Crow Eaters.* New Delhi; Penguin Books.

Sidhwa, Bapsi: *An American Brat.* New Delhi; Penguin Books; 1994.

Singh, Kushwant (translator): *Punjabi Poems of Amrita Pritam.* New Delhi; 2009.

3

Female Subjectivities and Relationships within Patriarchy

The term 'feminism' has been derived from the Latin word 'femina' meaning 'women'. The French dramatist Alexander Dumas coined the term feminism in 1872 which at present has been used and applied in different contexts and sub-texts. Feminism attributes to the issue of equality and women's rights movements, and further defines an intellectual, philosophical and political discourse directed at the issues of gender difference and legal protection for women.

In Western society, feminism has changed its outlook and perspective from culture to law. Feminist activists have campaigned or women's legal rights (rights of contract, property rights, voting rights) for women's right to bodily integrity and autonomy for abortion rights, and for reproductive rights (including access to contraception and quality parental care); for protection of women and girls from domestic violence, sexual harassment and rape; for workplace rights including maternity leave and equal pay; and against other forms discrimination.

Judith Astellana, in treating the subject the feminism, observes that it is a form of social transformation and movement that calls for an end of women's oppression. She traces the origin of the movement as a part of the long history of rebellion in an organized way expressing rebellion to the social institution that led to the subjection of women.

According to the ancient mythology of the world, it was believed that both the sexes had been one in the Creator, who was a perfect androgyme. Later the belief that Eve was merely built from a rib of Adam was simply a concoction to expound female subservience.

> The women's movement is merely the latest attempt to fulfill the objectives of orgasm, by which a man and a woman could cease to be known as such and instead become full person.
>
> (Kiberd, 1985:1)

For the above analysis of the lines, it is important to understand the conceptual distinction between femaleness, feminity and feminism. Femaleness refers to the physical and biological distinction between man and woman. Feminity refers to the social, cultural and psychological forms of gender bearing individual meanings. The various shades and forms of the construct of feminity emerge from the structuring of the society. Feminism describes an ideological position which works for the emancipation of women through cultural and structural transformation of society which aims to cease all forms of discrimination, oppression and exploitation of woman. This has been upholded and developed through women's movement to attain equality in genderally divisive world where as gender describes the various aspects of feminity; it is widely different from sex. Gender is a social construction while sex refers to what is biological.

> Each society slowly transforms a male or female into a man or woman, into masculine and feminine, with different qualities, behavior patterns, roles, responsibilities, rights...unlike sex which is biological, the gender identities of women and men are psychologically and socially—which means historically and culturally determined.
>
> (Bhasin, 2000:2)

Gender resists the discrimination between men and women explained on the biological level that sets the hierarchies of inequality that privilege men and disadvantage women. Gender does not take 'woman' and 'man' as separate identities but discussed its mutual interdependence on each other.

> During the 19th century the spread of industrialization led to promotion of the sexual division of labour based on the assumption that 'biology is destiny'. Woman's capacity to bear children began to be associated with her fixed role as caregivers and with it a host of psychological attributes like passivity, dependence moodiness began to be associated with it. In the economic and political sphere, the attainment of success were based on the biological notions of masculinity and feminity which further associated men's bodies and minds position of and women's to positions of subordination. Modern and contemporary feminism to an extent should be understood on this.
>
> (Eichenbaum and Orbach, 1992:67-70)

Mary Wollstonecraft (*A Vidication of the Rights of Women*, 1792), John Stnart Mill (*The Subjection of Women*, 1869), Margaret Sanger (*Women and the New Race,* 1920), Simone de Beauvoir (*The Second Sex*, 1949), Betty Friedan (*The Feminism Mystique*, 1974) and Bell Hooks (*Ain't I a Women*, 1981) are a list of feminists who have written about the causes and forms of women's oppression and have reconceptualized sexual differences in their writings. At present feminism continues in its endeavour to establish itself as the ground for women's political, economic and cultural ascendancy in the face of its own internal debates about the significance of differences among women.

Feminism is also interpreted as a critique which centralizes on the concept of patriarchy which can be explained as a male power which oppresses women through its social, political and economic institutions. Feminism can therefore be comprehended as a critique of patriarchy, on the one hand, and an ideology consigned to women's liberation on the other. Feminism as an ideology has branched out on various theoretical intersections—Marxist feminist, anarchist feminist, radical feminist, liberal feminist. Feminist methodology has its inception from a tradition of consciousness rising in the women's movement and by including women's experience it has created an important place in the field of methodological analysis.

To become a feminist is to possess a radically altered consciousness of oneself and feminists name this struggle as 'consciousness rising'. Sandra Lee Bartley points out

> feminist consciousness is also consciousness of victimization.

Lesbian groups, first and second wave Western feminism by black and Third World women have introduced many approaches within the feminist discourse. This has been further reinforced by feminism's association with post-structuralism and post-modernism.

In the light of contemporary world, the ideological place of feminist may be summed up in the words of Simone de Beavoire,

> She (woman) is defined and differentiated with reference to man and not he with reference to her; she is the incidental, the inessential as opposed to the essential. He is the subject, he is the Absolute—she is the other.
>
> (Beavoir, 1997:XVI)

The effect of feminism has led women, all over the social world, to identify with the feminist stand, voicing against this 'otherness'.

Feminism rose in the West and it delineates its various categories like Liberalism, Marxism, Socialism and black feminism. Feminism in India cannot be fixated into these categories nor it can follow a different path altogether. Indian feminism and Western feminism have always shared common theoretical positions and yet feminism in India claims and distinguishes itself from Western discourse. The variance assigns to the pre-colonial social structures of the Indian society and the role of women in it claims a different position for the Indian feminism.

The effect of colonialism on Indian culture and its effect on Indian womanhood through various social reform movements led to the mergence of nationalism with feminism in India.

Social values, historical circumstances and political construct of Indian society make women's issues different from the Western feminist rhetoric. This explains the critical distinction between Indian and Western discourses in feminism. While in India, the stature of Indian woman is inserted into its patriarchal structure through religion which ascertains traditional 'cultural spaces' to woman in India in their writings. The outcome of this change in attitude owes to a deep and intensive study of India woman—rural or urban, rich or poor, aristocratic or bourgeois, high caste or dalits.

In the middle of the 19th century, women's writing in English emerged after the introduction of 'antahpuras' into the lives of aristocratic liberal Indians.

In the time of India's struggle against the colonial power, from the time of Raja Ram Mohan Roy, issues related to women's life became an integral part within the male dominated culture. During the pre-independence period men like Dwarka Nath Tagore and Kashub Chandra Sen moulded the lives of women by bringing them out of *purdah* and by making them an important part of the nationalist struggle. By making women participate in small meeting with men they created new space for women in the Indian society. Bharat as name and Brahmo Samaj formed by Keshub Chandra Sen designed in creating a 'new' kind of 'women'.

So the first phase of Indian feminism (1850-1915) was started by men to curb such social evils like (sati, widow immolations) and to bring information in society through widow remarriage, promotion of literacy, prohibition of child marriage, and securing property right for women through law.

These changes that were witnessed by the Indian society were a part of the colonial venture brought through the concept of democracy, equality and individual rights. During this phase of feminism, women were bracketed with the low caste and treated as victims and subjects for social reform and welfare rather than being acknowledged as agents of change. Women were being recognized in newer form and roles other than there pre-existing feminine roles.

The second phase of feminism (1915-47) gained momentum when India's struggle for independence intensified and nationalism became the major cause in expanding and involving Indian women in public activities like the civil disobedience movement. Women took active participation in the various freedom struggle movements and Gandhi glorified the feminine roles of sacrifice like tolerance, self-abnegation and care. In this period, All India Women's Conference (AIWC) and the National Federation of Indian Women (NFIW) emerged. There active involvement in the freedom struggle kindled there analytical mind in understanding there role and rights in independent India. This led to the introduction of franchise and civic rights of women in the Indian Constitution.

In post-independent India, the third phase of feminism began from 1947 onwards. When the world embarked on a new wave of feminism, India also saw a new generation of Indian Feminists. Contemporary Indian feminists are voicing for equal pay, individual autonomy, abortion, breast feeding, and control of the female body, domestic violence, patriarchy, prostitution and many more. In the literacy filed such eminent writers like Amirita Pritam, Kusum Ansal and Sarojni Sahu are dwelling deep into the study of sexuality in relation to feminism. Medha Patkar, Madu Kishwar and Brinda Karat are feminist, social workers and politicians who are fighting for women's cause and struggling to gain legitimation for feelings, desires and lifestyle of women.

> Indian women novelists for almost the last six decades of post-colonial history of Indian English fiction have emerged victorious in moving forward to match the pace of the world. The transition and transformation in the social, political, and cultural backgrounds in India, is reflected in the literature of the modern times. It is in such a culture in recent times, that voice of dissent is heard against the traditional role of women in society from the strong advocates of women's right called feminists. One of the primal and seminal concerns of these advocates of feminism is to declare that a woman

> is an autonomous being capable of, through trial and error, finding her own way to salvation. They have protested against the relationship of sexes, where woman have been forced to occupy a secondary place, conditioned by strong cultural forces and social tradition.
>
> (Myles, 2006:90-98)

One of the reasons that women have in such large numbers, takes up their pens is that it has allowed them to create their own world. Similarly, so many women have taken to reading women's writing because it allows them a safe place from which they can explore a wide range of experience of the world, from which they can identify with a range of characters and a variety of existence. That is why women's writings have occupied such a significant and central place in their lives.

The introduction of women's studies in the academic curriculum is a step in the right direction. It is encouraging to note that women are entering the profession in a big way. In the present-day literacy world, there are several great creative writers in all Indian languages. A brief study of the Indian English male and female novelists may enable us to study the position of women in traditional Indian society, their slow conversion to modernity in the wake of women's literature movements and projection of "New Woman" by women novelists in the post-independence era.

> The new woman voices a note of dissent and resents being stifled under the oppressive restrictions. She has her own changed notions of life. It is true, woman's education, her rights of citizenship and other legal rights and above all her gainful employment and economic independence have tremendously influenced her outlook on conjugal relationship and attitude towards marriage. The new woman scripturally and factually denied of equality, freedom and opportunity has been struggling with the 'fury' of goddess 'Kali' to break her chains and incarnate a new avatar of womanhood. She is developing a new sensibility and consciousness which will no longer tolerate the suffocating familial, institutional, political

and cultural norms which place her in a humiliating subject status.

(Singh, 1998:45-50)

After the Second World War the history of Indian women novelists got a new track and new vision. In this period Kamalya Markandaya, Ruth Prawar Jhabvala are the most outstanding ones. Then come Nayantara Sahgal, Anita Desai, who herald a new era in the realm of psychological portrayal of the women character. Sashi Deshpande, Shobha Dey, Manju Kapur, Bharti Mukherjee, Arundhati Roy, Rama Mehta, Jhumpa Lahiri the other who have made their permanent mark in the field of English fiction. They are being conferred on not only national but international awards also. In most of their writings they have tried their best to free the female mentality from the age long control of male domination. The conflict between tradition and modernity finds a prominent place in the portrayal of women by women novelists. The tensions and anxieties of being modern in a traditional society have been overlooked by most male writers, who have mainly devoted their attention to broad social features that emerge in the course of gradual metamorphosis of the old order. But the women writers generally write about the existential predicament of individual woman. They project this problem through incompatible couples, acutely sensitive wives and dutiful husbands. Their fictional milieu is the India in transition with its cultural and ethical values in the melting pot. In their novels, one could sense the author's urge for way of living which would respond to the inner most yearning of the Indian woman for self-emancipation and self-dignity. These women novelists in English have tried to understand intimately their predicament of their female characters. They represent the welcome "creative release of the feminine sensibility" which began to emerge after the World War II. They are vexed by the sheltered over-protected life reserved for them and the condescending,

> discriminative attitude adopted towards them not only by the society but also by the family.
>
> (Singh, 2007:112-20)

Manju Kapur, Bapsi Sidhwa and Taslima Nasreen, the three legends amongst the best women writers of the Indian subcontinent have well articulated the feminist perspective in their distinctive novels.

Manju Kapur's novels *Difficult Daughters* and *A Married Woman* explore deeply the female psyche, her sexual radicalism, her defiance of the traditional norms and her new and changed perspective of her relationships. Kapur in her delineation of women characters have emphasized the limitations of women's lives, her incessant struggle with patriarchy and her endeavour to regenerate herself in a male-dominated world. Both these novels by Manju Kapur are exquisite examples of man-woman relationship which transgresses the traditional value system, but end up with to go against the established order and norms of society to appease her wants and savour freedom, but end up being victims of their own decisions and made to retreat or compromise with their circumstances.

The novel *Difficult Daughters* is a story about three generations of women—Kasturi, Virmati, and Ida and their distinctive approach in dealing with their lives. In the light of feminist theories, *Difficult Daughters* registers the experiences of women, especially in terms of their social, political and moral situation. The novel through its portrayal of the three women representative of the three generations probably questions the social construct and social relations.

Society imposing its own expectations and norms on women make it difficult for them to break free from the mountain of conventions and tradition. Kasturi living in pre-independence India is unable to rebel against the institution that have been observed by countless female generations before her and is therefore condemned to a life of constant child-bearing and mundane domesticity. She is deprived of even the thirst for self-fulfillment. Her objectification is complete to such an extent that even her right to question her own status as child bearer is denied to her, "'I will die if I have another child' said Kasturi desperately". Her frustration turns inward, wrapping her impression of the people around her, especially her errant daughter Virmati.

The idea that the right to give birth or to deny it is fundamentally a woman's personal issue is reassessed when Virmati despite wishing to bring a child into the world, is forced into an abortion.

> 'And now?' asked Swarna, looking at the shame on the face of the woman before her, whose family was to be feared, whose lover was invisible in her time of need, and who in the end had to turn to her....
>
> (Kapur, 1998:171)

The burning question is that women even if like Virmati, they have the courage to rebel against and escape from social tyranny and oppressive restrictions are still not seen as completely free individuals. Their bodies are not their own. Ida goes one step forward, where she gets a divorce and establishes her own independent identity. But her alienation from familial duty only leads to further disillusionment, despair and loneliness. In an attempt to overcome the emptiness of the present she reaches into the past to recapture ironically the lost time of her mother and grandmother even though this was a culture she had initially resisted.

> I was nothing, husbandless, childless. I felt myself hovering like a pencil notation on the margins of society.... Without the hindrance of her presence, I can sink into her past and make it mine. In searching for a woman I could know, I have pieced together material from memories....
>
> (*Ibid.*, 258)

On an intellectual ground, the three women characters are viewed with their own individual objectivity and reasoning. Kasturi in the pre-independence period is unaware and ignorant of the concept of education, as society's expectation from her and her own aspiration are only limited in the spectrum of being a wife and mother. She is a part of that traditional mould where a woman's ultimate happiness lies in her domesticity. For Kasturi, her niece, Shakuntala's education is insignificant and trivial because her unmarried status desolates her whole identity in Kasturi's eyes. In the same light for Kasturi, her daughter's education is never given so much prominence and her rebellious attitude is considered as a repercussion of her acquired education. Virmati's intellectuality is revealed from her desire for education, her estrangement from her mother and her unconventional life in the pursuit of it. Her zeal for learning is what primarily makes her important in Harish's life. But somewhere their romance makes it difficult for Virmati to justify her role as a student. Harish looks in Virmati for that intellectual companionship which his first wife is incapable of fulfilling.

> Let her wash my clothes, if she feels like it. It has nothing to do with me. I don't want a washer woman. I want a companion.
>
> (*Ibid.*, 201)

However, ironically after getting married to Harish, Virmati craves for that domesticity to which Ganga is bound.

> And? And—What? As your wife, am I to do nothing for you? Just be in your bed?
>
> (*Ibid.*)

Ida is portrayed in the post-independence period where woman can enjoy full liberty to pursue their education without any constraints. But ironically for Ida learning is the result of external compulsion. As her mother rebelled against enforced ignorance and sought to become educated in order to establish her individuality, so Ida finds education itself a burden from which she attempts to escape. It is an irony; too, that education does nothing for these women. Their status, the respect they are worthy of in society's eyes depends less on their level of learning and more on their level of domestic stability.

Virmati, as a second wife and hence trouble-maker and Ida as a divorced woman, are seen as morally defective and unworthy women.

In this light, the author expresses her uncertainty concerning the position of women in the Indian social scenario. No matter how much a woman attains her education, establishes her identity but her conventional domestic life is the only determinate on the basis of which a woman is evaluated and estimated. The novel also registers the rigidness of society on women and how they are stigmatized and disreputed if they do not pursue society's protocol and decorum. Manju Kapur in this novel also examines on which perfect combination of domestic bliss and intellectual fulfillment can ensure a woman's respect and happiness.

The novel *A Married Woman* (2002) is an outstanding effort by Manju Kapur to explore the conundrums of the social institution of marriage, the peculiar predicament of the heroine and the unusual twist with questions its very sustenance. *A Married Woman* is a story of Astha and her married life; the experience of futility which leads her to pursue a relationship with a person of the same sex. There is also an attempt made the writer to understand the psyche of woman, her dejection, despondency and struggle to attain, fulfillment and realize her own self in her marriage. The pivotal part of the book is what discusses Astha's relationship with Hemant focusing on an attempt to understand the variegations of wedlock and also gives the impression of how the relationship of wife and husband is becoming more and more complex in middle class Indian society. Her relationship with Hemant on the surface level supposedly seems to be a happy one because as a husband he fulfills Astha's physical, emotional, and material needs. But Astha's attempt to realize her own self and to attain her identity as an individual leaves her disillusioned and inwardly she from her established roles of mothering; from a school teacher, her interest in politics, and her desire to explore the aspects of herself it leaves her thwarted and disgruntled.

> As my wife, you think it proper to run around, abandoning home leaving the children to the servants?
>
> Astha went into familiar distress. As his wife? Was that all she was?
>
> (Kapur, 2002:188)

As a woman, she is primarily entrusted with responsibilities which are characterized as 'feminine'. Astha's interest in politics leads to her differences with Hemant. For Hemant, Astha's interest in these male-dominated areas, negates her role and identity of being a married woman. Her contact with Aijaz who is a social activist and a theatre artist inspires her to participate in political activities, where she gets acquainted with a outer reality quite opposite from the banality of her personal life. Aijaz here acts as a catalyst making Astha realize inadvertently her hidden and missed physical yearnings which were not fulfilled or realized in her routine sexual intimacies with Hemant.

> If an accidental brush against her knee was so dislocating what would anything else be?
>
> (*Ibid.*, 115)

On another front, Aijaz also makes her feel and acknowledge her power to think independently and voice her opinion on a burning political issue concerning the Babri Masjid and Ram Janambhoomi campaign.

> "...the curtain on Babri Masjid: Fact, Fiction and You."
>
> "It sounds like a bloody tract", said Hemant.
>
> Don't you like it? asked Astha sitting next to him in the front row. The title was mine. Aijaz thought it was a good one.
>
> (*Ibid.*, 116)

This ignition of interest in Astha helps her to explore her latent talents of being a writer and painter. Gradually in her quest to fulfill her identity and her varied interest and vocations occupies and moves her away from the ordinariness of her familial duties. This leads to her estrangement from her family. Astha and Hemant's quarrels and misunderstanding disbands Astha emotionally resulting in real health crisis.

Astha and Peepilika's relationship is viewed in the novel, as how a woman identifies with another in order to fulfill their physical and emotional inadequacies. Both the women in their lives feel disillusioned and unfulfilled, so their bonding with each other physically and emotionally nurtures a sense of belonging and circumvents their loneliness, giving them an opportunity to be their true self. Astha's attempt to evade from the mundaness of her marriage does not succeed as her innate bond with her family ties limits her to the boundary of her conventional marriage.

Her relationship with Peepilika can be explained in the light of the higher human urges which act as a refuge from her shattered family life. This urge comprises an important element to fulfill and satisfy her existence as an individual forgetting the guises of mother, wife and daughter. Their physical union is comprehended as the pure coalesce of mind and soul where they forget their personal pain and anguish.

> Privately Astha thought perhaps it was just as well...the disbanding of Pip's house, where they had been skin on skin, mind on mind with nothing in between.
>
> (*Ibid.*, 303)

For Peepilika, her lesbian relationship acts as an antidote to her personal tragedy of losing her husband and for Astha it serves as an act of vengeance on her husband who diminishes her identity of a woman. Astha is portrayed as Kapur's 'New Woman'

> conscious, introspective, educated wants to carve a life for herself, to some extent she even conveys a personal vision of womenhood by violating current social codes.
>
> (*Ibid.*, 217)

Astha and Aijaz in their relationship portray their selfless love and care for man, religion and society. Peepilika and Aijaz through their alliance represent their profane love and Astha and Peepilika have their lesbian affair.

Peepilika and Astha's affair exhibits a transgression but at the end, they move into their own shells without extending their expediency and retreating into their ordinary lives.

Manju Kapur's third novel *Home* (2006), adds one more laurel to her success as an eminent novelist in the Indo-Anglican literature. As the title of the novel is *Home*, the space of home is definitely identified with the women of the family, who are relegated to the four walls of their household.

The book tells an excellent story of a joint family, where each member is widely different from the other; yet their common roots make them nestle together. *Home* metaphorically represents the hopes, aspirations, disappointments, yearnings, mourning and fears of a family.

By *Home* the construct itself is matriarchal in nature and it delves deep into the feelings, which the womenfolk of the family happen to feel for each other. The book also draws on the writer's understanding of the uncertainty and inconstancy of human beings and their relationships.

The book opens with Lala Banwari Lal, his wife and two sons, running a cloth business in Karol Bagh. Though the novel circulates around this family, Kapur's prime focus is to highlight the power struggle between a mother-in-law (formerly the only mistress of the family) and her position shared when she gets a daughter-in-law. Related to this aspect of the book, Kapur has etched out the unchanged and stereotypical beliefs and attitudes of the mother-in-law of two successive generations. To analyze this power structure, the writer concentrates on 'Maji' (playing mother-in-law to Sona) and Sona (playing mother-in-law to Pooja). The faceless nature of women is exemplified by the epithet 'Maji' given to the senior most mother-in-law, who, throughout the course of her life in this household, is never referred to by her own name, but is seen simply as the patriarch's wife.

The first part of the novel marks out Maji's acid reactions against her son's independent decision to marry the girl of his choice.

> The thought of her favourite son entrapped by a clever manipulative, dowry less creature made it barely possible for her to look pleasant....
>
> (Kapur, 2006:8)

This highlights the norms of the patriarchal social order, where a woman imposes her authority and sustains her identity through such positions like mothering a son or by her wifely duties. Therefore, Yashpal's decision to marry Sona reveals his mother's sense of loss of that exalted position. In the second half of the book, Sona's son Raju and her daughter-in-law Pooja, are shown to enjoy their marital bliss. Raju and Pooja's involvement in each other is treated by Sona as the abandonment of a mother by her son,

> a new wife could take away in weeks what had been theirs all their life.
>
> (*Ibid.*, 8)

This again retells the same story where Maji felt the same insecurities and her position was threatened by her son's wife. Sona also suffers from the same isolation, when she gets Pooja, as the second mistress of the family to share her responsibilities and primarily her son. Sona says,

> Beta, you have forgotten you have a mother, a sister, a father, all for a wife of less than six months.
>
> (*Ibid.*, 11)

This draws on the present social institution, which is supported by cultural values and normative expectations, which force women to an unreasonably narrow role. It is the pernicious effect of this social conditioning, where a woman experiences a sense of extreme vulnerability and disintegration if she cannot hold on to some form of male support, whether it is husband or son.

Manju Kapur expresses her close sensitivity to typical female experiences through the portrayal of Nisha (Yashpal and Sona's daughter). Nisha's affair with Suresh is disapproved of by her parents, owing to Suresh's low status and class. This again draws on the traditional conventions of society which debar a woman from opting for her choice in marriage. Nisha's failed love affair makes her feel all the more helpless and cheated. Her helplessness converts into rebellion, which is expressed in her deep resentment for Pooja (her brother's wife) who is shown to be enjoying marital bliss. This expresses Nisha's craving for emotional security, love, and feeling of wholeness that a marriage with Suresh would have offered. It also conveys the typical feminine feelings which look for male support to nurture self and identity. In the later stage, Nisha's emancipation and success temporarily breaks this emotional dependence as after her marriage, it is her wifely duties and motherhood which gain a prerogative over her independent business venture. So it is the patriarchal tradition which has made women victims emotionally, physically and intellectually. This belief is well reflected, when Sona remains childless for the first ten years of her marriage. She is perpetually reminded of societal expectations from her and she becomes an object of pity and resentment.

Finally, when she becomes pregnant she receives all the care and attention from her family

> Always there was Sushila and mother-in-law asking questions carefully holding Sona's medical file, meticulously inserting the test report.
>
> (*Ibid.*, 105)

and it being reflected that a woman wins respect and adulation in a family, only when she performs her expected roles.

In the novel, when Sona is craving to become a mother, she is subjugated to the role of mothering Vicky. Her intense desire to mother a child, and her inner rebellion unable to accept Vicky as her child, shows her helplessness as a woman not able to fulfill her motherly instincts, and becoming a victim of enforced motherhood. We observe in the novel the detrimental effect of astrology in one's life. Nisha's *mangalik* status, from her birth is treated as a weapon to subjugate herself and complicate her life. A girl born under normal condition is forced to be considered unlucky in the institution of marriage, which makes Nisha choose a second best. Nisha's whole identity is made to look subservient by such an astrological set-up. Kapur treats this belief and interprets it in a negative light to portray the society's backwardness to enslave and oppress women.

> This was not good news, mangalis were horribly difficult to marry off. Unless they found a man with similarly unfortunate stars, unhappiness or death was the result.
>
> (*Ibid.*, 126)

One major concern that holds Kapur's writings is her ability to bring out some disturbing home truths which she narrates in her mature detached perspective. Vicky's sexual harassment of Nisha; raises and questions the definition of home. Home, which on the one hand is treated as an abode, where one seeks shelter from the outside world stands out for Nisha as a place which slurs her for life.

A place, which promises a sense of belonging to its inhabitants, can become the most unsafe and dangerous at the flick of a switch.

So the definition of 'Home' shows its ambiguity and its duplicate nature. In the text, when Vicky's sexual mistreatment of Nisha figured out by the elders of the family, she is shifted to her aunt's place. In this regard, the writer's objective is to picture the horrors of patriarchy which are not articulated in order to save the prestige and honour of the family.

A part of 'Home' which is created by the female members of the family, whose role entitle them to be an essence of it; the other half of it is built by the male members who act as the provider, protector and procreator of the family. As the book relates the story of a joint family, with Lala Banarasi Lal as the head, he is shown to be the pillar of the house. The aftermath of the partition makes him shift his home from

> Anrkalli, the famous commercial district of Lahore, to a camp in Amritsar, then Delhi, to finally arrive in Karol Bagh.
>
> (*Ibid.*, 155)

This feeling of homelessness which can be assessed as the most enervating and tortured experience of human beings, does not deter Banwari Lal's spirits and he recreates his new home and

> 'allowed no regret to weigh down at rebuilding' his family's lives.

Yashpal and Pyare Lal after their father's death hold on to the reign of their family. One important aspect of their role playing which the writer has tried to emphasize is their masculine power to subdue women and yield control and authority over their household.

It is this inheritance from the conditioning of patriarchy which sidelines the narrow politics of the female world; prevents the family from disintegrating and upholds the overall interest of the family.

In an interview, Bapsi Sidhwa remarked

> As a woman, one is always marginalized. I have worked among women to create an awareness of their rights and protested against repressive measures aimed at Pakistani women and minority communities....
>
> (Batulia, 2000:235)

First published in 1988 as *Ice-Candy-Man* and three years later under the title *Cracking India* (1991), Bapsi Sidhwa's novel was one of the firsts to gain wide attention to demonstrate the feminist concerns about women's issues, particularly their experience of victimization and suppression during the Partition period. The book is set at the backdrop of the nationalist movement in pre-Partition Lahore. Sidhwa's narrative of the Partition holocaust is presented through the innocent eyes of an eight year old Parsi girl, Lenny, who recounts her growth from her childhood to adolescence during the country's division. Quite different from the mainstream writings on Partition, which is basically hero-oriented, Bapsi Sidhwa takes women protagonists and weaves her novels representing their consciousness and psyche as affected by the political, social and cultural upheavals in society. This can be interpreted as an effort by women to make female protagonists as active survivors and resistors who act against the system.

Ice-Candy-Man is a novel which brings forth the diverse experiences of women belonging to different communities; their domestic lives, their individual features, their harrowing experiences of sexual exploitation, their resistance and their sexuality at the background of the Pakistani and Parsi ethos. The novel can be deftly approached as an effort in the genre of the women-centered writing, where assortments of characters bring out effectively the relationship between the two sexes in the society.

The prominent novels written on partition like *Train to Pakistan* by Khushwant Singh, *A Bend in the Ganges* by Manohar Malgoankar and *Azadi* by Chaman Nahal women have been portrayed as victims of communal riots. But *Ice-Candy-Man* sets a different example in representing the sufferings and agony of women during the traumatic event of partition. The book does not only narrate their heart-wrenching experiences but it also exhibit the strategies to surmount the inhuman atrocities at their personal level in handling their individual relationships with their male counterparts and at the social and national level.

Lenny, the eight-year-old protagonist of the novel also becomes a part of this picture and observes the intrinsic factionalism between a man and woman which raises her consciousness to understand the multiple ideologies which are gender related. Sidhwa in drawing Lenny's character has limited her range by making her physically 'handicapped' 'girl' child belonging to a religious minority but the limitation of the protagonist essentializes the content of the text by making her initiation in the adult world and placing the text within the parameters of women-centered narrative at the backdrop of the historic-political concerns.

Colonel Bharucha announcement, when Lenny goes for her medical treatment,

> She is doing fine without school...she does not need to become a professor.... She'll marry—have children lead a carefree life....
>
> (Sidhwa, 1988:15)

highlights the vulnerability and marginalization of women in his reconciliatory definition of a woman's being. The unacknowledged suffering of women, the writer records through the incident when in the clinic of Colonel Bharucha, a couple arrives to get their infant checked. Whenever the doctor asks a question regarding the infant's health the husband consult his wife,

> This time the woman addresses the doctor directly looking at him through the netting covering her eyes,

> "He vomits every time he has milk...five, six times a day". Her voice is incredibly young. She could not be more than twelve, I think, surprised.
>
> (*Ibid.*, 12)

This element of unexpectedness and shock expressed by the narrator hits on the silenced sufferings of women whether it is the twelve-year-old mother or the child-bride Papoo, whose lives are glamourised by appeasing statements spoken by Colonel Barucha. The girl child narrator in narrating her childhood experience arises as one of the effectual sources in understanding and exploring the female universe which are pulled in by the limiting and restricting forces of patriarchy and colonials. She begins her story on a pessimistic note,

> My world is compressed.... My child's mind is blocked by the gloom emanating from the wire-mesh.
>
> (*Ibid.*, 1)

The seven-year-old Lenny authorizes herself through her accusations, lucid pronouncements, and also her muteness. As the narrative progresses she becomes a subject to be moulded and educated.

> The covetous glances Ayah draws educate me....
>
> (*Ibid.*, 27)

The 'chocolate-brown and short' Ayah becomes an important link in introducing Lenny to the outside world. Her male admirers expressing their lustful love become a source of knowledge to her about sexuality.

Experiencing the pain of loneliness she gravitates towards her Godmother, for whom Lenny says,

> That bond that ties her strength to my weakness, my fierce demands to her nurturing, my trust to her capacity to contain that trust—and my loneliness to her compassion is stronger than the bond of motherhood. More satisfying than the ties between men and women.
>
> (*Ibid.*, 5)

She is led into sensing the feeling of romantic love; the meaning of male gaze and also experiencing the 'pitiless face of love'. She finds Ayah's sexual life quite pleasurable and entertaining in contrast to her mother's married life where in spite of being a dutiful wife, a good hostess, an attractive woman, she occupies a subservient position and tries hard to make her love recognized by her husband.

> Mother hates it when he covers his face: as if he is distancing himself from her even in his sleep.
>
> (*Ibid.*, 3)

Lenny observes her mother's behaviour critically and realizes her incessant efforts to ill up the incompleteness in her marital relationship. She overplays her roles and responsibilities in order to win her husband's heart. She concocts stories to "fill up the infernal time of father's mute meals". Sidhwa artistically etches out the mother's character and skillfully delineates her character as she goes, she goes through the same feminist concerns and predicaments even after belonging to the economically privileged strata of society. Though she is relieved of the domestic responsibilities of rearing children and socializing, she blames herself for not gratifying her motherly responsibilities properly.

> "I don't know where I went wrong", she says "It's my fault.... I neglected her—left her to the care of Ayah. None of the other children who went to the same park contracted polio."
>
> (*Ibid.*, 22)

This reiterates the pressure and responsibilities of socially constructed gender 'duties' that a mother is expected to fulfill. But the mother's new 'role' as a social worker during the partition trauma, to rehabilitate the victims of partition across the allotted nations, makes Lenny realize the true purpose of her mother's endeavourers. Sidhwa brings out this dichotomy by showing the mother being exploited in the domestic sphere but preserving her individuality in the midst of that exploitation.

Lenny is acquainted with the larger concerns of society, community, nation, sexuality and the trauma of partition as she moves around with her Ayah. The small world of Lenny expands as she comes in contact with the outside world through her and the book resonates with the historic-political concerns and its global prospective.

Lenny's Ayah and her mother share many resemblances in their roles and responsibilities. While being the nanny of Lenny she is paid for her motherly functions and she even realizes like Lenny's mother that to gain importance in a man's world she needs to submit herself to their ways. In the Victoria Garden she is surrounded with a company of male admirers including the Ice-Candy-Man, a masseur, a gardener, a restaurant owner, a zoo attendant, a knife sharpening Pathan and many more. She is aware of her own positioning in the gender divided world and she cleverly manipulates her sexuality to fulfill her small desires. Her maneuvers and artifice of survival is enjoyed by her though it reasserts her exploitation in a patriarchal set-up. She uses her sexuality by making her wooers go one against the other and winning favours from them. Her sexual endeavours make Lenny differentiate between physical desire, romantic love and animal lust. Lenny says

> Ayah is nervous in his presence given to sudden movement,... His presence radiates warmth that is different from the dark heat generated by Masseur's fingers—the lightning—strikes of Ice-Candy-Man's toes.
>
> (*Ibid.*, 75)

Lenny's observation of Ayah's engagement with her male admirers awakens her to her own feminity and she becomes mindful of her bodily developments

> I look about me with new eyes. The world is a throb with men. As long as they have some pleasing attribute—height, width or beauty of face—no man is too old to attract me.... I finally permit my lover to lay his hand upon my lover to lay his hand upon my chest. It is no small bestowal of favour, for my chest is no longer flat.
>
> (*Ibid.*, 219)

She learns to guard her body from male touch, "I can't trust anyone" and becomes cautious from her cousin who always look for a chance to touch her while it can be ascertained that Lenny's confinement is not in respect to patriarchal norms as to her being a handicap. Zoroastrianism too does not believe in the concept of 'purdah or *female segregation into zenana* or Andar Mahal'.

But being in a Muslim-dominated area, and observing its tenets Parsee women have to live a constricted life. In telling contrast to Lenny who enjoys the freedom to move around the world with her nanny, is Papoo, who is ill-fated to be born in such a class and caste that she has to marry Tota Ram,

> A dark, middle-aged man with pockmark-pitted face... has an insouciant air of insolence about him.... I cannot take my eyes off him as he scrutinizes the women with assertive, assessing directness.
>
> (*Ibid.*, 109)

Papoo becomes a prey of the oppressive patriarchal social structure and it outlines the precarious nature of women's position in society.

At this juncture, Ayah also becomes an untold victim of the partition holocaust. She is kidnapped, raped and pushed into the Kothas by the Ice-Candy Man. The masseur is also murdered under communal hatred and this ends Ayah's love-story.

The Ice-Candy Man's repeated protestation of love fails to win Ayah's love and reinstate her faith and spirit. Lenny is withdrawn to see Ayah

> Where have the radiance and the animation gone? Can the soul be extracted from its living body? Her vacant eyes are bigger than ever....
>
> (*Ibid.*, 260)

Ayah moves back to her family in Amritsar with Godmother's hard efforts but the narrator is uncertain about her fate and her capacity to deal with the blemish of being a 'fallen woman'. Thus, the central ethos of communalism working within the patriarchal structure of power is the woman's body that expresses a woman's weakness and perishability that calls for feminist concerns and debates.

Hamida and Ayah become the signifiers of shame and subjection of a community and their brutal rape is identified not as a violation of womanhood but an attack on the manhood of the community.

Bapsi Sidhwa's *An American Brat* (1993) is just another of her classics. The book discusses the journey of a sixteen-year-old Feroza's rendezvous with three cultures—her own Parsee culture; secondly the Islamic culture which her stay in Pakistan acquaints her with and later her move to the Western culture of USA. Unlike her other novels, *An American Brat* is a serious study to understand and explore the differences between the two worlds—namely the First and the Third World; the three cultures—Parsee, Muslim and Western culture respectively; and between the two generations of people 'the mother and the daughter'.

The narrative resolves around a Parsee girl Feroza Ginwalla, who is sent from an increasingly fundamentalist state of Pakistan to America to be liberated from her unprogressive and conservative attitudes,

> In the car she said: Mummy please don't come to school dressed like that; she objected to my sleeveless sari-blouse.
>
> (*Sidhwa*, 1994:11)

As the novel travels from one location to the other, the characters, their situations and their perspective also meets with gradual transformation. The book studies the three cultures in its intricacies and it also etches out the predicament of the individuals who undergo this cultural adaptation. Feroza, a Parsee girl is born and brought up in Pakistan. Being a Parsee, her stay in an Islamic cultural set-up makes her indoctrinated with political and religious beliefs of Islam. As women are conditioned by a society, their status at home and outside is determined and shaped by its cultural ethos; the extreme conservatism spreading throughout Pakistan, make her mother send her to visit her young uncle, Manek, a student in America.

> "I think Feroza must get away" Zareen continued, "Just for three or four months...travel will broaden her outlook, get this puritanical rubbish out of her head"
>
> (*Ibid.*, 15)

Sidhwa artistically hits on the restrictions imposed by the society which relegates a woman to her domestic life (to the boundary of her house) and is forced to occupy a secondary place, conditioned by strong cultural forces and social tradition. Zareen's effort to send her daughter to America is an attempt made to free her daughter from the limiting norms of patriarchy and her conditioning into passivity.

> Women mustn't show their legs, women should not dress like this and women should not act like that. Girls must not play hockey or sing or dance...and stay within the four walls of their houses.
>
> (*Ibid.*, 10)

The novel examines the three worlds and Feroza's experiences in three cultures. Zareen being a Parsee epitomizes the Parsee culture and emits the sense of flexibility and freedom expressed by it.

> Look we are Parsee, everybody knows we dress differently.... When I was her age, I wore frocks and cycled to Kennaird.
>
> (*Ibid.*, 11)

Feroza resisting her native culture, follows the Islamic culture, and subjects herself to the conundrums of its traditions. Her stay in America allows her to explore the American culture, and she gradually accepts and embraces it. The set up of American culture induces a sense of freedom and liberation in Feroza and she determines to marry David Press, an American jew.

The decision to marry outside Parsee culture though fulfills and sustains her identity of being the 'New Woman', yet it disclaims her from being an obedient and dutiful daughter. The familial pressure not to marry outside the Parsee community is intimidating to her family as Zareen accepts the loss of identity faced by them, which eventually leads to lessen and disintegrate the members of the Parsee community in these inter-community weddings.

> Mixed marriages concerned the entire Parsee community, and affected its very survival. God knew, they were few enough.... Parsees were a gravely endangered species.
>
> (*Ibid.*, 268)

Feroza's mother Zareen whose identity and sense of self-worth is derived mainly from her role as a wife and mother is severely affected by Feroza's decision to marry David as being a mother she is over-involved and over-identifies herself with her child. Consequently, when Feroza fails to meet her need of what Zareen considers 'good' marriages she is unable to gratify her role of a mother and experiences a sense of worthlessness. As Zareen says to Feroza

> You are robbing us of a dimension of joy we have a right to expect. What will you bring to the family if you marry this David?
>
> (*Ibid.*, 278)

In order to foil David and Zareen's marriage plans, Zareen goes to America, where inadvertently she develops a liking towards David. The complexities of racism and cultural separation do not stop Zareen from liking David. Zareen herself becomes conscious of the precepts of universal feminism that flows beneath various cultures, societies and temperaments. She understands the differing cultural, economic, and political spheres, where women are less valued than men as she reflects,

> ...how unfair it was that while a Parsee man who married a 'non' could keep up his faith and bring up his children as Zoroastrian, a Parsee woman could not. And it did not make sense that the 'non' was not permitted to become Zoroastrian, one could hardly expect their children to practice a faith denied to their mother.
>
> (*Ibid.*, 287)

Zareen soon revises her position and stands distressed by letters received from home and she sets herself on the original task to free her daughter from David. At the end, she becomes successful in dissuading David to break his relationship with her daughter on the pretext of their cultural differences. Bapsi Sidhwa in plotting this end has shown the power of the socio-cultural ethos over human emotions and feelings. Probably, David realizes the importance of his religious beliefs and culture in which he has been brought up, which he could not abandon or change after marrying a Parsee girl. This apprehension and fear allows David to forgo his relationship with Feroza. Sidhwa's second novel *The Pakistani Bride* published in the year 1983 is a work which extols the writer's feminine sensibilities; her preoccupation with women's inner world and articulately bring out the existential predicament of women as individual. Her exploration in different societies and communities make her fathom the plight of women in a tribal society in Pakistan through this book. The book is a poignant illustration of struggle between adherence to customs and traditions and the courage and fortitude of a woman spirit. Like in other works, this book also documents the terrible events of partition of the Indian subcontinent in 1947 at the background. The central figure of the text Zaitoon, is portrayed as a victim of the communal riot; losing her parents in it and adopted by Quasim, a tribesman who brings her up as his daughter in the bustling city of Lahore.

The background created by Sidhwa in this novel brings out the ethos of a Islamic society which is quite typical of Sidhwa's writing. Being cared by Mariam, Zaitoon starts to grasp the moral beliefs and practices of this culture, where she understands the significance of a woman's body which stands as a symbol of communal dignity. Mariam says

> You are now a woman. Don't play with boys—and don't allow any man to touch you. This is why I wear burkha.
>
> (Sidhwa, 1990:55)

The socio-cultural construct of a society basically foregrounds the attributes and positioning of women in society. In this way, a woman is conditioned first to marriage and then to procreation, an inevitable gendering and generalization of the society.

> Bringing out this aspect Zaitoon is pictured, at the centre of this. Marriages were the high points in the life of the women as she grew older Zaitoon became an eager participant in the activity centered around them.
>
> (*Ibid.*, 89)

The socially constructed roles and behaviour assigned to women make Zaitoon an object of sacrifice for Quasim. Quasim in a fit of nostalgia agrees to marry her to a man of his tribe in mountains.

Zaitoon's romantic imagination and allusion make her agree to this, but upon reaching Koistan and meeting her husband she realizes she will never fit into tribal society.

> Abba, 'she begged in a fierce whisper, take me
>
> Back I'll look after you always....
>
> (*Ibid.*, 156)

Her contempt for the place and her fondness for Ashiq Hussain, a jawan of the Pakistani army, arises her against the injustice but later she reconciles with the situation. Her initial cry for freedom is curbed by the forces of patriarchy; here exemplified in her father. Quasim rebukes Zaitoon and says

> Hush, Zaitoon, that's no way to speak to your father. It is not seemly. A decent girl does not tell her father to whom he should marry.
>
> (*Ibid.*, 158)

The cultural conditioning and the structural patterning of the society make Sakhi the causative factor inflicting pain on Zaitoon, making her vulnerable to suffering. Zaitoon's initial inability to comprehend the ways of tribal life makes her susceptible to Sakhi's anger and wrath. Her shift from a civilized city life to a life of harsh existence in the barren hills of Himalayas; her leap into her married life make her efface herself and is emboldened as her husband's honour.

Sakhi's initial attempt to comfort Zaitoon is categorized by his male counterparts as his subjugation of male supremacy and power. Unable to withstand this shame and humiliation on his manliness, he torments Zaitoon to the extent that she becomes immune to her ostracized life.

> In his presence she drifted into a stupor, until nothing really hurt her. He beat her on the slightest pretext. She no longer romance. She now lived only to placate him.
>
> (*Ibid.*, 174)

Sidhwa in drawing the nuances of the Islamic society has described sexuality, love, yearnings, sexual fulfillment and procreation an area of shame, confinement, distress and enforcement, for women.

Zaitoon undergoes the same, where her identity and self is completely obliterated by her changed status in life. Her marriage becomes an indissoluble bond which subdues and reconciles her to her unavoidable duty and inevitable fate. She becomes a substance of patriarchal exploitation of marriage which make her realize,

> and two months into her marriage an incident convinced her she might not live that long.
>
> (*Ibid.*, 175)

Viewed objectively Zaitoon is first made the symbol of her father's honour and later she becomes the pride and honour of her husband. In becoming this metaphorical symbol, Zaitoon becomes an object who is led to sacrifice her.

Running parallel to Zaitoon's story, the writer has scripted the story of Carol, a white woman living in Pakistan. Carol falls in love with Farukh, and eventually settles in Dubair.

Carol the second 'Pakistani Bride' in the novel, does adapt to the place well,

> I love Lahore; it's beautiful and ram shackled, ancient and intensely human....
>
> (*Ibid.*, 108)

but she remains quite casual about the stringent customs and practices of the society. Carol's conduct and deportment becomes a reason for Farukh's humiliation and dishonour, as according to him she seems to flout the imperatives of the cultural ethics and morals.

> I am so ashamed of you! Displaying your honky-tonk pedigree. You laugh too loudly. You touch men....
>
> (*Ibid.*, 108)

Society's hypocrisy is exposed as it proves to be tolerant towards Carol, but at the same time is severe against women like Zaitoon and Hamida.

> One of the pleasant surprises of her marriage to Farukh was her very special status. As an American married to a Pakistani she was allowed much more freedom than a wife.
>
> (*Ibid.*, 218)

Belonging to a different race, though exempts Carol from wearing a burkha, or living in segregation; she becomes an object who is disregarded as an individual and becomes a substance of enjoyment and gratification for others.

> Carol's face hardened. Three tribesmen had stopped on the track looking down at her...their eyes examined her insolently.
>
> (*Ibid.*, 112)

Farukh's jealousy and possessiveness seems to breed in Carol a sense of retaliation which leads her astray. At the same time, Zaitoon's sense of disbandment from her place and family augments in her a sense of disbandment and longing. Carol and Zaitoon's escape from their troubled life make Carol think of her marriage to the Major, whereas Zaitoon opts to flee from her ostracized existence.

Carol's first meeting with Zareen seems to strike an untold secret which they share with each other. Carol realizes on Zaitoon's behalf the convoluted ways of married life which awaits her.

> ...an understanding they shared of their vulnerabilities as women. For an intuitive instant Carol felt herself submerged in the helpless drift of Zaitoon's life.
>
> (*Ibid.*, 136)

Zaitoon's efforts to pull herself from her ostracized existence do mark the projection of 'New Woman' fighting against patriarchal monopoly and control. She removes herself from the authoritarianism and protection of the patriarchal family. Her saviour at the end of the novel establishes her power and defiance to fight against the patriarchal set-up that leads to suffering and subjugation of women.

Bapsi Sidhwa's novel *Water* (2006) documents widows' lives in Banaras, at the backdrop of the pre-independence period. The novel opens with Chuyia's mother and father giving consent to her marriage to a man few years younger than her father. This shows how men and women are complicit in upholding the traditional fundamental structure of a society which is willfully ignorant of the repercussions of such an ill-match. The death of Chuyia's husband leads to her disbandment from her family and she is forcefully sent to a widow's ashram in Banaras. Her widowhood seizes from her the tokens offered to her in the name of matrimony.

> The smashing of the bangles was the first of many rituals designed to mark Chuyia's descent into widowhood.
>
> (Sidhwa, 2006:33)

Sidhwa artistically evokes the helplessness of an eight-year-old child, victimized by the inhumane social tradition which looks upon a woman's widowhood as a more serious matter than the death of the man.

> She trotted the newly-minted widow out like a doll she had dressed up for all to see and glorified in their attention as the mildly shocked mourners turned to stare sympathetically at the comely little widow.
>
> (*Ibid.*, 34)

Chuyia's husband's death metaphorically signifies her social death and like all widows she pays the penalty of her existence, by not being treated as a part of the social milieu. Like all widows, she is insulted, ill-treated, shaved, ill-fed and taunted. She is abandoned in an ashram in Banaras, a shelter for widows.

But gradually Chuyia befriends the other women of the ashram and overcomes her sense of dislocation. Her youthfulness and babyish activities bring a new jest of life in the ashram and she is fondly called 'a little mouse'. Here Sidhwa has tried to make Chuyia act as an instrument that evokes the simple desires and yearnings of women who are shunned for life time.

Shakuntala's motherly attachment to Chuyia reveals her heartfelt desire to mother a child and fulfill her motherly instincts which inadvertently also gratifies her search for wholeness.

Kalyani seeks a friend and sister in Chuyia who helps her to give voice to her unexpressed love. She becomes a medium through which Kalyani relives her youth and dreams of settling down with Narayan. So Chuyia's emerges as a means for these women to give expressions to their shattered feelings which they are forbidden to reveal.

In characterizing Madhumati, Sidhwa has drawn the inhuman and torturous side of the patriarchal practices which has made a woman its puppet. The widows who are expected to lead a life of celibacy after the death of their husbands and are portrayed as models of chastity and purity are forced into prostitution for their sheer existence.

> We must live in purity, to die in purity, said Madhumati disregarding the hypocrisy in preaching this to a young woman forced into prostitution against her will.
>
> (*Ibid.*, 144)

This exposes the hypocrisy of a society which on the one hand treats widows as objects of contempt and is consequently considered taboo on society, is secretly used by upper-caste men to satiate their physical hunger. This impiety of the magnified social structure of Hinduism becomes more glaring through the projection of Madhumati and Gulabi who force the widow in this sex-act.

Kalyani (a young widow) when falls in love with Narayan, a Gandhian idealist, their love affair defies the norms of the traditional social structure and threatens to inviolate the codes of widowhood. Kalyani's attempt to seek to fulfillment in her romantic love affair is soon thwarted, when she comes to know about Narayan's father who seeked his physical fulfillment in Kalyani taking her as a prostitute. This again sweeps in the element of satire against the social construct of the society. But paradoxically it also brings in an element of contrast by showing a change in the outlook of two respective generations. Narayan's father stands for a society which is responsible for the degradation of women whereas Narayan stands for a society which is trying to overcome traditional biases and is working towards a humane attempt to protect women from the devastating torments of widowhood.

Kalayani's death at the end of the novel exhibits the dark vicious circle of the period which left no outlet for widows to seek an alternative from their vulnerable and oppressive existence.

> Kalayani knew she had no choice: there was only one avenue open to her. Caste out in the streets she would die but to live without Narayan and return to a life of forced prostitution would be a worse kind of death.
>
> (*Ibid.*, 177)

This reinforces the idea that if widows were not debarred from remarriages, it could have secured families from disgrace and infamy and diminishes the crimes of prostitution.

> She must have known of his tawdry infidelities: how could she tolerates them? He knew at the same time that she had no option but to....
>
> (*Ibid.*, 174)

The dark and morbid side of the story reaches to its climax when Chuyia is forced into this sex trade. But Shakuntala's efforts save her from this menace and finally she is sent with Gandhiji and becomes a part of his entourage. The book ends on a positive note and enlightens hope of the possible rescue of widows from the torturous and oppressive practices of Hindu tradition. It is a new start with the emergence of a new class with new sensibilities working for the freedom of women to deliver them from all bondages.

> I know I shall face more and more problems. But I shall continue my battle till my last breath.

These lines are spoken by one of the most famous and controversial writers Taslima Nasreen. Nasreen a staunch feminist and humanist, through her book *Lajja* (1993), make a breach in the boundaries created by the socially constructed silences that women are supposed to observe. *Lajja* with reference to feminist approach bespeaks about the indignities, anguish and pain suffered by women in a society which is infested with the virus of communalism.

The book scripts the story of the inhuman sufferings of a Hindu family that is terrorized at the hands of Muslim fundamentalists. The title *Lajja* meaning 'shame' is consequential as it wrings out shame from its cultural, social and political being and consciousness. The ban imposed on the book exclaims the untrammeled revelation of a society that is crushed by religious dogmatism. The book projects the dauntless courage of a woman writer who protests against the appalling violation of human rights, engendered on a minority community.

In basing the story, the writer has intertwined religion and sexuality, placing women at the centre of it. The women character in *Lajja*—Kironmoyee and Maya—have been subjected to utter fear and haplessness because of their being in a minority community and it is intensified by their belonging to a gender which positions them as 'inferior', 'passive' or 'subordinate' in comparison to men.

The communal hatred raised by the demolition of Babri Masjid in India, effectuate their ordeal and predicament in Bangladesh.

Suranjan's escape to her muslim friend's house during the riot discusses her earnest urge to save her life.

> I see a definite change in Maya. Perhaps the desire to survive will compel her to change her name....
>
> (Nasreen, 1993:74)

As the writer has merged religion with sexuality; she has made it quite evident in the treatment meted out to Maya on her arrival to Calcutta. She being an inhabitant of Bangladesh is distanced by the members of her extended family in India making her feel alienated and marginalized. In this case, her national identity estranges and demeans her and her religious identity is nullified and disowned.

> She had found her cousins vain and egoistical and she was looked down upon by them. They would never invite her to join in their activities.
>
> (*Ibid.*, 68)

Kironmoyee's abandonment of

> using sindur in the parting in her hair and Loha and sankha on her wrists....
>
> (*Ibid.*, 97)

explains that the external religious signifiers becomes a part of one's identity and Kironmoyee's inability to wear it proclaims her unwilling acceptance of the other religious custom.

The institution of marriage is treated as a religious weapon that finalizes the complete subversion of one's emotion and identity. Suranjan's refusal to convert to Islam is treated by Parveen as his denial of his love for her,

> No, you must become a Muslim. I don't want to be a Muslim which means, you don't want me either.
>
> (*Ibid.*, 111)

As Suranjan's conversion is considered as a natural and an essential vocation which would have sanctified their marriage contract.

At the backdrop of the communal violence, Kironmoyee emerges out to be a true figure of patience, self-sacrifice, love and care that construct and maintain the cult of true womanhood.

> He was amazed at the way his mother held the family together. She never complained about anyone....
>
> (*Ibid.*, 107)

She has been portrayed as a woman who is inescapably trapped in a social morass but not resigning from her duties and responsibilities. She has been characterized as an ideal wife and mother, becoming an allegorical figure representing all that is resilient and strong.

The barbaric and the most inhumane act of the riots have been described by the writer, when Sudhomoy is incapacited to "make a Muslim out of him". Assessing the event from a feminist perspective one notices how Kironmoyee dissociates herself physically from her natural feminine urges and does not try to justify feminine sexuality with feminine imperatives.

> She would never leave him, ever. After all, was sex the only significant aspect of a relationship between a man and a woman? Was everything else insignificant?
>
> (*Ibid.*, 114)

Kironmoyee fosters the image of ideal motherhood, where she fulfills her maternal role of taking care and protecting her children from all odds. She upholds the figure of a silent, self-effacing and self-abnegating mother who annihilates herself in the process of redeeming her family.

Her womanhood bears the brunt of the communal violence as she suffers as a woman, wife and a mother. Her victimization meets a decisive end when her home ransacked and her daughter Maya is kidnapped by Muslim communalists. This evokes an extreme sense of loss, pain and helplessness in her, subjecting her motherhood to a deep sense of trauma and mourning. Maya's abduction and her assumed rape and death in the narrative, shows the anger and wrath that is directed against the desecration of a woman's body, indicating the victory of one community over the other. So it can be assessed that a woman's body is treated as pawn, in the communal war, whereas her sexual purity marks the patriarchal honour and its violation defiles female sexuality, dishonouring her community and religion.

The outcome of this catastrophe emerges out in the form of Suranjan's raping a prostitute of the Muslim community. As a prostitute, the woman is already stigmatized and denounced in society and her rape expresses his avenge on the other community. The violence accompanied with it symbolizes his domination over another community emphasizing its humiliation.

References

Beauvoir, Simone De: *The Second Sex*. UK; Random House; 1997.

Bhasin, Kamala: *Understanding Gender*. New Delhi; Kali for Women; 2000.

Eichenbaum, Luise and Susie Orbach: *Understanding Women*. England; Penguin Books; 1992.

Kapur, Manju: *Difficult Daughters*. New Delhi; Faber and Faber, 1998.

Kapur, Manju: *A Married Woman*. New Delhi; India Ink (Roli Books), 2002.

Kapur, Manju: *Home*. New Delhi; Random House India; 2006.

Kiberd, Declan: *Men and Feminism in Modern Literature*. Delhi; Macmillan Press; 1985.

Myles, Anita: *Feminism and the Post-Modern India*. Delhi, Sarup & Sons; 2006.

Nasrin, Taslima: *Lajja*. New Delhi; Penguin Books, 1993.

Sidhwa, Bapsi, Butalia Urvashi: *History Workshop Journal*, Delhi; Oxford University Press, Autumn 2000.

Sidhwa, Bapsi: *Ice-Candy-Man*. New Delhi; Penguin Books, 1988.

Sidhwa, Bapsi: *The Pakistani Bride*. New Delhi; Penguin Books; 1990.

Sidhwa, Bapsi: *The Crow Eaters*. New Delhi; Penguin Books; 1980.

Sidhwa, Bapsi: *An American Brat*. New Delhi; Penguin Books; 1994.

Sidhwa, Bapsi: *Water*. New Delhi; Penguin Vikings; 2006.

Singh, Jyoti: *Indian Women Novelists*. Delhi; Rawat Publication; 2007.

Singh, Charu Sheel: *Women about Women in Indian Literature in English*. New Delhi; Anmol Publication; 1998.

Swain, S.P.: *The Feminine Voice in Indian Fiction*, Delhi; Asia Book Club; 2000.

4

Locations of Culture and Society

The Indian subcontinent or the South Asian subcontinent comprises the countries of India, Pakistan and Bangladesh and it also includes Nepal, Bhutan, Sri Lanka and Maldives. For a very long time, the Indian subcontinent was known for its commercial and cultural wealth. It has been the birth-place of the four major religions, namely Hinduism, Buddhism, Jainism and Sikhism, whereas Zoroastrianism, Judaism, Christianity and Islam came in the first millennium and gave a new face to its diverse culture.

India gets its name from Indus, which originates from the Old Persian word *Hindu*, from Sanskrit *Sindhu*, the historical signifier for the Indus River. Hindustan a synonymous word for India is derived from a Persian word for *'Land of the Hindus'* used to refer the whole of India.

India was colonized by the British East India Company from the early eighteenth century and by United Kingdom from the mid-nineteenth century. India gained its independence on 15 August 1947. Meanwhile the Partition of India was done by British India on the ground of religion that led to the creation of the sovereign states of the Dominion of Pakistan (later Islamic Republic of Pakistan) and People's Republic of Bangladesh and the Union of India (later Republic of India) (Ramakrishna, 2005:10-15).

The division was proclaimed by the Indian Independence Act of 1947 and led to the dissolution of the British Indian

Empire. The Bengal province was geographically divided into East Pakistan and West Bengal (India) and the Punjab province was divided into West Punjab (later Punjab Pakistan and Islamabad Capital territory) and East Punjab (later Punjab India), Haryana and Himachal Pradesh.

The partition of India in 1947, though made a move towards the creation of the two nations, but was appended by massive transfer of population and entailed mass killings, rape, sexual assault and unprecedented violence.

It is to be noted that the conception of India as a nation took shape through the anti-colonial struggle for independence. The memories and the recollection of the constitution of the nation take place through its representation in memoirs, mythologies, songs, literature and films. These sources add to the significance, which led to the formation of a nation. They project the social and cultural ethos of that period of time imparting to the historical meaningfulness of the moment. The partition of the country led to the creation of an imagined nation that was later called as Pakistan and which invariably caused to the re-narration of the nation describing the various steps structuring it.

Expounding the term culture in relation to India, it is taken into consideration that culture is defined by religion, language, regional and ethnic communities that describe its being. Colonial India has characterized itself with religion, religious reform movements and at the end of the 19th century it visualized itself as a Hindu India. In the words of Swami Vivekananda,

> The one common ground that we have is our sacred tradition, our religion. That is the only common ground, and upon that we shall have to built.... The unity in religion therefore is absolutely necessary as the first condition of the future of India
>
> (Prasad, 1994: 164)

This definitely limits the concept of nation and can be reasoned out to be a consequence to resist colonial hegemony and the influence of English education that initiated the process of self-alienation.

Gandhi in his *Hind Swaraj* (1908) expanded the term stating that

> In reality there are as many religions as there are individuals; but those who are conscious of the spirit of nationality do not interfere with one another's religion. If they do, they are not fit to be considered a nation. If the Hindus believe that India should be peopled only by Hindu, they are living in a dreamland.
>
> (Gandhi, 1938:44-45)

Bankim Chandra Chatterjee's *Ananda Math* (1882) and Raja Rao's *Kanthapura* which acquired the status of national classics have tried to reflect and grasped the crux of the problems in it.

> During the second half of the nineteenth century, Indian writers of different languages like Bankim Chandra (Bengali), Narmada (Gujarati), Bhartendu Harishchandra (Hindi), and Vishnu Shastri Chiplunkar (Marathi) used their historical consciousness as a means to give expression to the political and social issues of their region. The writers played multiple roles of social and religious reformer, novelist, poet, political activist, journalist, essayist and many more in this attempt.
>
> (Kapadia, Dodiya: 2001:100-05)

Novels can be regarded as the most vital source of history. In the other way round, history is equally cherished by novels as it is displayed by the works of many Indian English novelists. In the first half of the nineteenth century, the Indian English novelists focused on the national and social issues concerning the freedom struggle. The Indian English novels at that period of time have dealt either with the freedom struggle or in portraying the ideology of Gandhi and created the background of most of the novels.

The triumvirate, R.K. Narayan, Mulk Raj Anand and Raja Rao are the novelists of the first phase of the Indian English novels who captured the socio-political events around them and exemplified it in their fictional works. The historical incidents inspire them to work with their literary representations but their works do not bear any direct engagement with it. The national and social concerns many a time have encouraged writers to reconstruct their novels surrounding the lives and deeds of real heroes.

Novelists have written about the partition, days of terror and violence that people suffered which further consolidates and narrates a nation's history and its ideology. Partition as an event has led to a specific social and cultural change of the nation. This change which was caused by violence, bloodshed, and forced dislocation has directly made an impact on the society and culture of the nation. Partition narratives have inspired fiction and historical accounts that have espoused the cultural, social and historical discourses. These discourses revolutionized literature at its core and reflected the pain and the acts of brutality of their communities in various historical and fictional narratives.

The women writers of the three countries, namely Manju Kapur, Bapsi Sidhwa and Taslima Nasreen have taken the genre of Partition novels and presented their individual perceptivity on the communal divide accompanied with it the sense of dislocation, loss and the emotional turmoil of the characters. The event of Partition has been taken as the backdrop to set their stories and to delineate their characters' lives. How the geographical division of the country has outlined and occasioned the birth of different communities from one have been dealt by the writers. What has been a common thread in the writings of the three novelists is that they have projected violence that accompanied partition as the inevitable and the most logical outcome of communal tensions.

> December 1940. Congress leaders in the Satyagraha movement are arrested on a daily basis. Their names appear in the papers, and if their prison centres are changed their names appear again.
>
> (Kapur, 1998:124)

> The swollen gunny-sack lies directly in our path. Hari pushes it with his foot. The sack slowly topples over and

> Masseur spills out—half on the dusty sidewalk, half on the gritty tarmac—dispelling the stiletto reek of violence with the smell of fresh roses.
>
> (Sidhwa, 1988:174)

> But this evening, my brother-in-law came and told me that in Manikgunj city and in the police station area, more than a hundred homes had been looted and burned. Twenty-five temples were torched. In a village called Bokjhuri, all the Hindu homes were burnt down. Also, in the middle of the night they barged into Deben Shore's house, dragged out his daughter Saraswati and raped her.
>
> (Nasreen, 1993:40)

The politics of partition accompanied with the massacres of partition evoked a serious change on the social, political and national outlook of the nation. Partition enunciated the knowledge of Muslims being the perpetrators of violence and the cause of danger to the nation. This view and the notion of Muslims being the cause of the Partition have been denounced by Sidhwa. Her portrayal of the Pakistani life, society and culture gives a new representation to the national ideology of Pakistan and lays the ground of creating a particular interpretation of Muslim identity.

In *Ice-Candy-Man,* Sidhwa uses a lot of Urdu poetry that has influenced her.

> Shall I hear the lament of the nightingale, submissively lending my ear?
>
> Am I the rose to suffer its cry in silence year after year?
>
> The fire of verses gives me courage and bids me no more to be faint.
>
> With...God I make my complaint.
>
> (Sidhwa, 1988:1)

In order to make the cultural differences evident, Sidhwa has used untranslated Urdu words like the political slogans *Jai Hind Jai Hind* and *Pakistan Zindabad* (p. 127), *'lungi'* (p. 127), *janab* (p. 129), *hakim* (p. 61).

She uses Urdu poetry and Urdu language to create the 'Muslimness' of the text and to represent the Muslim identity. When the ice-candy-man recites verses from Zauq, Faiz, Iqbal and Mirza Galib, it brings back the aura of Urdu culture and language.

> Why did you make a home in my heart? Inhabit it. Both the house and I are desolate. Am I a thief that your watchman stop me? Tell me I know this man. He is my fate.
>
> (Sidhwa, 1988:277)

Manju Kapur has brought in the words of Punjabi, which become the marker of the culture and region of North India. She has also used untranslated Punjabi words like *praji* (p. 13), *shor-shaar, uthala* (p. 1), *phenji* (p. 17), and *palla* (p. 16).

Though Taslima Nasreen's work *'Lajja'* is translated into English, the language, style and the identity of the characters signify the culture and social life of Bangladesh.

> He had been quite young and after eating sweets at a shop he had asked the shopkeeper for some water. The word he had used was paani, not the word he would have normally used, jal, for at that time hostilities between the Hindus and the Muslims had been high.
>
> (Nasreen, 1993:180)

Manju Kapur, Bapsi Sidhwa and Taslima Nasreen have revolved their narratives around the institution of marriage, which has received social recognition and approval in all cultures and in all times. The institution of marriage which is treated as an ideal and sacrosanct form of social existence is exalted in all civilized social organization. However, the commonality that is felt in the writings of the three novelists is that they have signified marriage as a patriarchal attribute that decides the complete suppression and defeat of women's identity.

As Beauvoir observes,

> Marriage is the destiny traditionally offered to women by society. (Beauvoir, 1997:444)

The institution of marriage adjudges her code of behaviour and establishes the picture of ideal feminity. The conditioning of patriarchy offers no substitute to marriage and condemns those who try to thwart it.

The conventionalities of Indian society place the community above the individual. In the Indian social structure, the legacy of tradition and cultural mores portray women as a token of veneration and is expected to comply with all that the mythological figures like Sita, Gandhari, Savitri and Parvati symbolize.

Women's fictions too portray the traditional image of women in her institutionalized roles within the limits of the institution of marriage. They also depict the sufferings of women due to their blind allegiance to the archetypal codes and precepts which denigrates their basic virtues.

In *Difficult Daughters,* Ganga, the professor's second wife is pictured in her traditional role which circles around her husband,

> From washing his clothes to polishing his shoes, to tidying his desk, dusting his precious books, filling his fountain pens with ink, putting his records back in his jackets, mending his clothes, stitching his shirts and kurtas, hemming his dhotis, seeing that they were properly starched—Ganga did it all.
>
> (Kapur, 1998: 216)

On the other hand, Harish does not value her wife's domestic roles and is totally indifferent to this,

> She's a housewife, you know. Somebody has to do these things.
>
> (*Ibid.*, 216)

For Ganga, her husband's second marriage is a big blow for her but she is unable to articulate her strong feelings of opposition to this settlement. Her economic dependence on her husband and the traditional moral codes of behaviour silence her repulsion in deep pain.

> The tears Ganga was determined not to show anybody started pouring down her face. She buried her face between her raised knees, and wept as though he heart would break.
>
> (*Ibid.*, 211)

She accepts her husband's rejection of her but still holds on to him considering him to be her God and to never have a

> thought that did not pertain to his well being.
>
> (*Ibid.*, 242)

The patriarchal exploitation of marriage is observed in such cases where the women's allegiance to their virtues and traditional roles subjugates and devalues them. They become a victim of patriarchal monopoly but try to correlate with patriarchy in the maintenance of this institution.

Kasturi in *Difficult Daughters* is portrayed in her stereotype role as a wife within the confines of marriage. Her sufferings evoke from her acceptance to fulfill her husband's wishes. She conditions herself to self-denial, self-obliteration and in service of others. This also displays the feminine requirement for external self-validation which will project her in the traditional image of an 'ideal wife'.

> Kasturi could not remember a time when she was not tired when her feet and legs did not ache.... Her teeth bled when she chewed her morning neem twigs, and she could feel some of it shaking. She had filled the house as her in-laws had wanted, but with another child there would be nothing left of her.
>
> (Kapur, 1998: 7)

This highlights the pattern of the Indian social structure that believes in subjugating and sublimating women in conformation to the norms of the society. In the tradition-bound patriarchal Indian community, a woman has to accept and practice the principles that the community lays down.

Though Virmati, in all her efforts try to assert her individual freedom by rejecting the traditional ways of life, she remains unhappy and fails to merge herself into the community.

By defying the norms of society, she is treated as an outcaste. She is unable to escape from the pangs of guilt and finally she succumbs to it, exclaiming as a sign of protest,

> I break my engagement because of you, blacken my family's name, am locked up inside my house, get sent to Lahore because no one knows what to do with me. Here I am in a position of being your secret wife, full of shame wondering what people will say if they find out,...
>
> (Kapur, 1998:137)

Virmati, too, demand for her independent identity but she has to submit herself to the dominant discourse by being a traditional wife.

Manju Kapur has woven her stories at the background of Indian society portraying the Indian culture and its ethics honestly and realistically. In the novel *A Married Woman,* she has uniquely presented the idea of feminist community at the backdrop of the Indian society. Defining a new borne phenomenon, Kapur has taken the context of lesbianism which though considered as a stigma has been presented as a weapon for rebellion against the present value system.

Women writers from India, within their distinct area of the temporal and cultural constructs, are representing the varied forms of bonding from sisterhood to homosexual relationships. This explores their strategies which confirm their desire to see change in the traditional Indian society.

Kapur has shown the lesbian relationship between Astha and Pipeelika as a bonding between two women who are mutually dependent on each other. The homosexual bonding in this relationship offers solace to physically, emotionally and socially battered women.

> 'Why did you then? You want to spoil what we have.'
>
> 'I had thought that with a woman it would be different-
> 'So did I. With a woman.'
>
> (*Ibid.*, 268)

Kapur in exploring the relationship outside a husband and wife does not try to negate or undermine the socially acknowledged relationships. The Indian writers' cultural conditioning and their grounding in a hegemonic ideology will not permit them to go against the mainstream truisms, so its only a few writers who have initiated to delve into these forms of reality which a traditional society refuses to accept.

Islamic society is largely a patriarchal, patrilineal system. In the context of tradition-bound patriarchal Muslim community, an individual has to follow and accept to certain principles that the community lays down.

Though *Quran*, preaches equality among men and women, the system practices male supremacy on women. The *Quran* makes men,

> 'the managers of the affairs of women', requiring righteous women to be 'obedient, guarding the secret for God's guarding', advising women to 'cast down their eyes, guard their private parts and reveal not their adornment...save to their husbands'.
>
> (Moghissi, 1999:22)

The basis of Islamic culture lies on complementarity and not equality. This complementarity is based on biological determinism which accords a man to be leader and provider and a woman as a child-bearer and nurturer. The basic biological difference confines a woman to a subordinate position and it functions intensely on a social, familial and personal level.

In Islamic societies, the women's body is treated as an object for procreation and as a symbol of communal honour. Therefore, it is veiled and bounded. A woman's body is trained for defiance and is also destroyed (sanctioned legally and culturally) in anticipation of encroaching. The code of moral beliefs and practices of Islamic societies hold a woman to be weak-minded in moral judgments and imperfect in cognitive capacity.

Islamic laws related to marriage and divorce express women's inability to enjoy a rightful legal status. The marriage contract and its cancellation are arranged between the male citizen and state. In case of marriage, the father plays an important role and husband, in case of divorce. The concept of *Shari'a* forbids a woman to enter a marriage, contract without the permission of her father or guardian. *Mehr* empowers the fathers to legally marry-off their daughters for a set amount and authorizes a man to terminate a marriage-contract without the approval of his wife. The efforts to bring about changes in the Qur'anic ideologies have done little to improve the personal standing of women.

Islam stands highly in contrast to other traditional religions specifically, to both Judaism and Christianity. Judaism and Christianity celebrate celibacy and virginity as they consider marriage a worldly obligation and condemn any kind of sex that does not lead to reproduction. Sexual union only for pleasure is treated as a sin.

On the other hand, Islam does not support celibacy. The Prophet is believed to have propounded marriage for Muslims, that is, equivalent to half of his religion.

> Marriage shields them from 'promiscuity, adultery, fornication, homosexuality', and is commendable 'even for person who has strong will to control his sexual desire, who has no wish to have children, and who feels that marriage will keep him away from his devotion to Allah'.
>
> (*Ibid.*)

Islam negates celibacy and celebrates sexual pleasure as a lawful right of its believer.

> Eternally lasting physical pleasure and unrestricted access to the female body as the source of physical pleasure would be delivered to the believing man in Paradise as rewards for his piety, good deeds and self-control in life.
>
> (*Ibid.*)

Islamic orthodox beliefs view women as an object of sex and justify sexual hierarchy. Though Islam equally recognizes female sexual drives and women's right to sexual fulfillment, yet it is assumed that a Muslim man's sexual urges cannot be satisfied with one woman. Therefore, he is entitled to marry four women and the institution of *mut'a* allows him to keep as many temporary wives he can afford.

Islam denounces solitary sex and severely punishes homosexuality therefore; marriage is regarded as the only way through which a woman can seek sexual pleasure.

Islamic culture enforces sexual, moral and ethical codes that are strictly executed. In Islamic tradition, the spiritual leaders have been the law maker and administrator of the happenings of the Muslim community.

> Islam, however, is the religion as well as a legal and political tradition.
>
> (*Ibid.*, 26)

The predicament of women in the Islamic cultures owes to the historical, political, economic and social parochialism of Islamic societies and its expression in patriarchal cultural customs that ordains the religious dictation over the lives of the women. The relatedness of religion and politics with law and policymakers, religious-spiritual leaders has stifled the already weakened civil society.

Bapsi Sidhwa born in Karachi in 1938, moved to the United States in 1983, and lived in Charleston, Atlanta, Houston, Cambridge and New York. It is essential to mention the writer's multiple locales to get a better understanding of her use of the diverse cultural contacts that brings out the concepts of 'otherness', 'marginality', 'colonialism', 'interculturalism', and 'cultural hybridity' in her novels.

Sidhwa is a postcolonial author who approaches the aspects of cultural identity and cultural differences, very capably in her novel *The Pakistani Bride* (1981). The plot of the story narrates the events leading to an ill-arranged marriage between Zaitoon (who is brought up in the city of Lahore) to Sakhi, a Kohistani tribesman, (belonging to the mountains of Kohistan). The story very deftly brings out the emergence of the newly created Pakistan after the geographical and social division of the Indian subcontinent.

Quasim, a Kohistani tribesman, brings up Zaitoon (a survivor of the communal riots) in the bustling city of Lahore.

> Perched on his shoulders, captivated by the intriguing odours of fish frying in the Shalmi, of barbecuing liver and kabab, smiling at the colourful pageant thronging the streets and pouring out of cinemas, Zaitoon relished all his interests.
>
> (Sidhwa, 1990:47)

Though she is raised in the free and liberal city of Lahore, Quasim marries her off to Sakhi, a youth from his own tribe whose temperament and disposition is very different from his daughter. Even Mariam's consistent persuasion does not deter Quasim from his decision. Overlooking the harsh and difficult life that his daughter may have to lead; Quasim sacrifices her in the name of being a devoted and loyal member of his community.

> Sister Miriam, it is not for the goats and maize, please believe me. It is my word—the word of a Kohistani!
>
> (*Ibid.*, 94)

Sidhwa in describing the social structure of Lahore and Kohistan, bring out effectively the contrast and variance between the two locations. Lahore, being a vibrant and lively place,

> Kohistan has no administration. It is inhabited by isolated pockets of feuding tribes, for centuries imprisoned by the Karakoram Range. They have their own notions of honour and revenge; ...a man's pride slighted, and the price paid in bloody family feuds.
>
> (*Ibid.*, 115)

Through this she expresses the strong relation between community, religion, class to cultural identity and social structure. They not only mirror and affect one another but are also totally interconnected.

Zaitoon is unable to fit herself in the crude and harsh life of Kohistan. Her child-like innocence gets corroded in the strict and rigid atmosphere of the mountains. Her status of the newlywed bride is thwarted by the brazenness and savageness of her husband, quite intrinsic of the people and the place.

Zaitoon, not able to meet the norms and behaviour of the tribal tradition, has to face the cruelty and brutality of her husband.

The power and authority ascribed to the men of the community, makes Sakhi mighty and all-powerful to exercise his control on her.

> He was mortified by his bride's tempestuous display before all his kinsfolk. His voice was level but his grubby fingers bit vengefully into her flesh....
>
> (*Ibid.*, 168)

Sakhi's abusiveness and ability to inflict pain on Zaitoon may appear to be heroic for him and for his tribe; it emerges out to be a perennial source of sorrow and unhappiness for the women of the tribe. For the code of honourable behaviour women are treated worse than slaves and their lives solely revolve around serving their husbands. Women imagined being the figures of purity and chastity is brutally killed if they are suspected of being unchaste.

Sidhwa in portraying the tradition and value system of the tribe effectively articulates the misery and wretchedness of the women who happen to be a part of such community. As Sakhi's mother says,

> Honour! She thought bitterly. Everything for honour and another life lost! Her loved ones dead and now the girl she was beginning to hold so dear sacrificed. She knew the infallibility of the mountain huntsmen.
>
> (*Ibid.*, 109)

The sub-plot essays Carol's story, an American who is married to Farruk, a Pakistani engineer. The sub-plot gives us a chance to peep into the American culture and the subsequent cultural conflict that the character faces.

The ingrained social pattern of the Muslim society demanded Carol's subjugation and subservience.

> It had corroded her innocence, stripped her, layer by layer, of civilized American niceties. She was frightened to see a part of herself change into a hideously vulgar person.
>
> (*Ibid.*, 111)

Her notion of personal freedom and space is looked down upon and it is curbed and restricted by Farruk, in allegiance to the norms of his tradition.

Both Carol and Zaitoon discard the moulds of patriarchy by breaking the society's and their husband's moral codes and finally leaves them.

Sidhwa is a Parsi Zoroastrian and as an author her background plays an important role in her novels. In her three novels: *The Crow Eaters* (1978), *Ice-Candy-Man* (1988) and *An American Brat* (1994) she portrays the Parsi community and Parsi ethos and describes the historical perspective of this minority community.

The word Parsi conveys a native of *Fars* which is an ancient Persian province named 'Persepolis' in Southern Iran. Twelve hundred years ago, the Parsis left their motherland to save their religion and the teachings of Zoroaster, from being Islamized by the invading Islamic Arabians in the seventh century A.D. Their religion and philosophy is based on the teachings of Zoraster, founded in the early parts of the fifth century BCE. Zoroastrianism, the term signifies the worship of *Ahura Mazda* regarded by Zoroaster the supreme divine authority.

The religious text of the Parsis is known as *Avesta* and the heart of the religion can be felt in the five *gathas* or divine songs of Zarathushtra. The *gathas,* are the Prophet's dialogue with God, which describe the moral and righteous nature of his gospel.

In the Indian subcontinent, the Parsis are an ethno-religious minority who has settled in the west coast of the subcontinent, especially in Mumbai. In Pakistan, the Parsis have settled in Karachi and Lahore. Zarathushtra preached the monotheistic religion of one supreme god, *Ahura Mazda.* The teachings of Zarathushtra state that the whole universe is governed by two chief forces, good and evil. Individuals have to choose between *Spenta Mainyu* the strength of light and good and *Angra Mainyu* which stands for the evil spirits. Parsi Zoroastrianism believes in three moral demands—*Hvarshta* (good deeds), *Hukhta* (good words), and *Humanta* (good thoughts). According to Zarathustra's teachings, the clash between good and evil will lead eventually to the destruction of evil. Finally, it will lead to the restoration of universal peace.

In *Ice-Candy-Man,* the Parsi characters have been majorly influenced by the teachings of Zoroastrianism. During the riots, the narrator's mother, Mrs Sethi and her aunt Minnie go out to the trapped families of the minority Hindus and Sikhs, with cans of petrol, to help them escape across the border. Lenny's mother says,

> I wish I'd told you. We were only smuggling the rationed petrol to help our Hindu and Sikh friends to run away. And also for the convoys to send kidnapped women, like your ayah, to their families across the border.
>
> (Sidhwa, 1988:242)

The inspiration behind such noble and generous activity of Lenny's mother is neither individual valour nor to win political favour. Rather, the inspiring cause for such humane act can be associated to the Zoroastrian principle of 'good deeds'.

At the end of the novel, one of Lenny's aunts named Rodabai, displays remarkable efficacy and capability to deal a critical situation by rescuing the *ayah*, who was kidnapped and kept at a *kotha.* Rodabhai makes arrangement to keep the *ayah* in a rescued woman's camp and later sends her to a relative in Amritsar. Her benevolent act can be described by the Zoroastrian philosophy of noble thoughts and good deeds.

A historical outlook is important to explain the perplexity, identity crises and the issues of the Parsi community, which is aptly reflected in the novels of Bapsi Sidhwa.

In the eighth century A.D., the Parsis who are the descendents of the Persian Zoroastrians sought refuge in India, when Persia was conquered by the Arabs invaders. The battle of Nahawand in 642 A.D. led to the downfall of the Persian Empire and the Arabs started converting the people who were practicing the monotheistic religion of Zoroastrianism into Islam. As a result of this, many Zoroastrians absconded from Iran and took shelter in India.

Sidhwa in creating history in *Ice-Candy-Man* presents it, not only from the Pakistani perspective but also from the Parsi point of view. Explaining the Parsi dilemma at the time of Partition, she goes back to the Parsi history,

> When we were kicked out of Persia by the Arabs thirteen hundred years ago.... "We got into boats and sailed to India".
>
> (Sidhwa, 37)
>
> Our forefathers and foremothers waited for four days.... Then at last, the Grand Vazir appeared on deck with a glass of milk filled to the brim.... "It was a polite message from the Indian Prince meaning: 'No you are not welcome'...."
>
> "Our forefathers carefully stirred a teaspoon of sugar into the milk and sent it back...". "The Prince understood what that meant. The refugees would get absorbed into his country like sugar in the milk".
>
> (*Ibid.*, 38-39)

This short account highlights the dilemma of the Parsis over centuries of assimilating themselves into a foreign culture and the crisis of losing their identity. The event of Partition resulted to their confusion of showing allegiance to any three of the dominant communities/religions in India—Hindus, Muslims and Sikhs. The novel analyses this crisis at the backdrop, where Sidhwa brings to light their predicament during the partition of the country.

> Hindus, Muslims and even Sikhs are going to jockey for power: and if you jokers jump into the middle you'll be mangled into chutney!
>
> (*Ibid.*, 36)

Their alienation from all the major communities and their efforts to retain their individual identity forces them to arrive at the conclusion, where Col. Bharucha says

> "Let whoever wishes rule! Hindu, Muslim, Sikh, Christian! We will abide by the rules of their land!".... "As long as we do not interfere we have nothing to fear! As long as we respect the customs of our rulers—as we always have—we will be all right! Ahura Mazda has looked after us for thirteen hundred years: he will look after us for another thirteen hundred!"
>
> (*Ibid.*, 39)

Thus, Sidhwa articulates their stance of remaining impersonal and unaligned to the context of Partition and in all circumstances to preserve their culture and identity.

In the novel *An American Brat*, the Parsi community is depicted being actively participating in Pakistani politics. Though stating the intensity of the political effect on the masses, it becomes mandatory for them to be a part of it.

> In Pakistan, politics concerned everyone.... Because it personally affected everyone, particularly women, determining how they should dress, whether they should play hockey in school or not.
>
> (Sidhwa, 1994:171)

Feroza, though being in America identifies herself with Pakistani politics and as a citizen of that country she considers her right to be aware of the political scene. This brings out Parsi community's innate power of adaptability to accept a foreign country as their own motherland, though equally being protective about their own credos.

The Parsi-Zoroastrians are popular for being a very adaptable minority community. After their settlement in the Indian subcontinent, they have adopted Gujarati as their main language. With the coming of the British Empire, they were the first community to learn English. The religious texts of the Parsis are scripted in the ancient *Avestan* languages or the *Pahlava* script. In the present time, the Parsis are learning the speaking, writing and reading skills in the regional languages as well as in Hindi, English and Gujarati. Therefore, we witness the linguistic diversity in the works of Bapsi Sidhwa. A wide range of vocabulary used by the author is punctuated with Gujarati and Urdu words. Words like *Shahbash* (p. 245), *Khut putli* (p. 222), *Chachi* (p. 208), *Paijee* (p. 226) and *Churidar* (p. 105) have been used by Sidhwa in *Ice-Candy-Man.*

Her first novel *The Crow Eaters* (1978) is described by the author herself in the Preface as,

> The hilarious saga of a Parsi family.... Because of a deep-rooted admiration for my diminishing community—and an enormous affection for it—this work of fiction has been a labour of love.
>
> (Sidhwa, 1978: Preface)

The novel is ingrained with Parsi outlook, customs, values and behaviour. The novel starts with Faredoon Junglewalla's inherent loyalty to the British Empire which originates from the Zoroastrian religious belief of devotion towards their rulers.

> Next to the nawabs, rajas and princelings, we are the greatest toadies of the British Empire.
>
> (*Ibid.*, 12)

Freddy, after his arrival to Lahore,

> thus paid his homage to the British Empire, established his credentials and demonstrated his loyalty to Queen and Crown....
>
> (*Ibid.*, 22)

By this act, Freddy secures his identity, peace and economic prosperity. Sidhwa depicts the fear of identity crisis faced by this minority community by Freedy's sense of belongingness towards his own folk. His eagerness to meet the people of his community displays his affection and solicitude towards them and an earnest effort to maintain his identity in a land of diverse cultures and religions.

> An endearing feature of this microscopic merchant community was its compelling sense of duty and

> obligation towards other Parsis. Like one large close-knit family, they assisted each other, sharing success and rallying to support failure.
>
> (*Ibid.*, 21)

It also highlights that these hybrid subjects through their power to negotiate create their own zone of ease in their adopted homeland and cherish memories of their old home.

The book minutely details the mores, habits, customs, and rituals of the Parsi community. It allows the readers to have a full view of the life of Parsis, lived in an adopted country and in a plural community.

> Parsis are a tiny community who leave their dead in open-roofed enclosures atop hills—to be devoured by vultures.
>
> (*Ibid.*, 45)
>
> Beneath the self, on the prayer table, burnt the holy lamp with a likeness of the Prophet Zarathustra stamped on its glass shade.
>
> (*Ibid.*, 52)
>
> Visiting Parsis were rare. When they did steam into the city station the community mood became festive. The Toddywallas, the Bankwallas, Chaiwallas...vied with each other in making the visitors welcome. They were wafted from home to home for breakfast, brunch, lunch, drinks and dinner.
>
> (*Ibid.*)

Though the novel explores all aspects of Parsi community, the writer never divulges in attacking any of the behaviour and sentiments of the community. According to Makarand R. Paranjape,

> *The Crow Eaters* is not a novel particularly about Parsis; instead, it is a novel where characters happen to be Parsis. The characters could well have been Hindu, or Muslim and a good deal of satire would still have carried; each ethnic group, after all, has its peculiarities and absurdist.

An American Brat talks about multiple diasporas of Parsi characters, foregrounding the feelings of alienation, identifying with the adopted countries, suiting to the powers relationship between the majority and the minority and the cultural conflict faced in their host society. Categorizing the above idea into one, *An American Brat* falls in the genre of Diaspora literature. Apart from the elements of Diaspora, the book manifests the culture longing and the psychological alienation of the characters in the foreign countries.

Feroza, a Parsi, settles in Pakistan but is uprooted and placed in America, as it is known as a land of liberal traditions. Finding the Islamic codes of behaviour, usurping the Parsi ethos and the increasing fundamentalism of Islamic community, her mother comes to this settlement of sending her daughter to America.

> What I could in '59 and '60, my daughter can't do in 1978! Our Parsee children in Lahore won't know how to mix with Parsee kids in Karachi or Bombay.
>
> (Sidhwa, 1994:11)

The distance geographical and cultural arise a new set of feelings in Feroza. For Feroza, the changed geographical sites as her new place of being, leads to a constant tension between the old and the new homes and continues to simmer under the routine practice of negotiating between day-to-day life and identity. Feroza oscillates between two conditions of either to assimilate herself in the foreign culture or to accept her marginal status in her host country.

> Something within Feroza must have changed imperceptibly, because suddenly one spring evening Feroza discovered that the boys were talking to her, making a concerted effort to kid cajole and encourage her out of her painful shell.
>
> (*Ibid.*, 163)

Feroza's movement to a new nation and culture, her affiliation shifts to a new way of being and that directs her course of life in America. Her acceptance of the strict culture and tradition of Islam is metamorphosed in her encounter with a new culture of America.

Feroza's relationship with David, an American Jew is frantically disapproved by Zareen. Though accepting the liberal tradition and openness of American society, she is unable to give consent to Feroza's match, with a person who belongs from the same community. This shows the closeness and insularity of the community which does not permit a Parsi to marry a 'non' Parsi man.

Sidhwa also highlights the resistance of the community to convert either. This expresses the rigidity of the Parsi culture which is constantly trying to maintain its identity, banning inter-faith marriages. This also explains the individual's deep and subconscious bonding with the tradition, culture, religion, philosophy and language that Zareen does not wish to subtract for her daughter with her marriage to David.

> Zareen knew what she must do. However admirable and appealing David was..., he would deprive her daughter of her faith, her heritage, her family, and her community.... Cut off from her culture and her surroundings like a fish in shallow waters....
>
> (*Ibid.*, 289)

Indian civilization has its roots in Arabian, Persian, European, Buddhist, Christian, Dravidian, Muslim, Mongolian, and Aryan and assimilation of many other civilizations.

> The Indian subcontinent does not merely stand for a geographical entity. It refers to a civilization—the Indian civilization—that has evolved over the ages and is signified by various historical changes. The India subcontinent before its partition had two religious communities that had serious differences in their attitude. The British colonial rule took advantage of this and the division of the subcontinent led to the creation of the two separate states of India and Pakistan. Again in the state of Pakistan, the probable growth of the Bengali culture was being restricted. The outcome was that

> regardless the most inhumane genocide in recent history (inflicted by Pakistan), the emergence of Bangladesh could not be stopped. This subcontinent had observed conflict between two religions or areas. The region of the state had also experienced alteration and reconstructions. Unless the territorial and political unrest put the very human life at stake, civilization retains its identity and crust through the prolong act of construction of the political territory. Thus, in spite of many differences and variety in language, culture and religions the oneness and individuality of the Indian civilization is still maintained.
>
> (Jain, 2007:283-89)

The factors that lead to the changes and transformation of the territory of the state owes to many reasons. It can be explained aligned with other factors that the casteist and parochial view of the Hindu society was accountable for the formation of a separate Muslim country. But, on the other hand, the Muslims trace the origin of their culture and civilization in Arab culture rather than to the Indian civilization. If we study the language and culture of Arabia and Persia, we deduce that though they relate to Islam, they have never abandoned the pre-Islamic culture from their lives. They have imbibed the Islamic codes but have maintained their Arabian, Iranian, and Turkish identities as well.

Amongst the Bengali (Muslims), we witness this apprehension and anxiety in the way of this process; even though they have to agree to their Indian lineage in the realm of language and culture—including the faculty of arts and intellectual quest. Geographically, Bangladesh is an integral part of the Indian subcontinent, to which no one can disagree. A section of the Muslims in the subcontinent and Bangladesh cherish an anti-India outlook which owes to the historical conflicts with the Hindus. Regarding the civilizational identity of the Bengali Muslims; they suffer from the fear and anxiety that until and unless they discard their association with India and Hinduism, they will be devoured by the hegemonic Hindu culture.

> This is why, though they form 85 percent of the population in Bangladesh, they share the minority phobia that has been created across the sub-continent. It is this phobia that had once tried to impose Urdu and prohibit singing of Tagore songs in Pakistan; the recent symptoms include the bill on state religion, imposition of the Arabic language in school, introduction of religious education, preponderance of madras as and maqtabs, rehabilitation of jamat...and aversion towards Indian scholarship and so on.
>
> (Momen, 1999:12)

Taslima Nasrin (born 25 August 1962, in Mymensingh, Bangladesh) is a globally famed Bengali Bangladeshi writer. She has risen to the ladder of popularity through her radical feminist views and her assessment of Islam and of religion in general. She is a staunch supporter and spokesperson of secular humanism, gender equality, freedom of expression and a defender of human rights.

Her novel *Lajja* or *Shame* was published in 1993. Her other famous novel is *French Lover* (2002). Owing to her radical and revolutionary views on religion, she has been living in exile since 1994.

She started with her literary career publishing poetry from 1986 to 1993, dealing with the theme of female subjectivity and oppression. Her novel *Lajja* projected her as a serious writer, in which she has dealt with Islamic religious laws and Islamic fundamentalists.

Pakistan and Bangladesh are Islamic states. *Lajja* documents the story of a Hindu family in Bangladesh, at the background of the demolition of the Babri Masjid on December 6, 1992. Nasrin describes that period of history in her novel, when Bangladesh was fuming in the heat of religious fundamentalism.

Tradition, customs, rituals, values, myths and folklore, religion, philosophy and language define a culture and make a community. These cultural constructs are the platform that moulds the identity, behaviour and philosophy of life. *Lajja* depicts a gory side of a social construct, that is, religious fundamentalism. The author essays the crisis and tribulations of a nation that is torn apart by religious fundamentalism.

> Almost 50,000 Hindus in no less than 10,000 families have been finished off completely. Mobs set fire to their homes, after looting and plundering everything they could find off any value. At least 500 million takas worth of property has been lost, two people have died and two hundred have been hurt.
>
> (Nasreen, 1993:71)

Lajja documents the story of a Hindu family in Bangladesh at the background of the demolition of the Babri Masjid on December 6, 1992. Probably after the publication of the novel, Taslima Nasrin became an iconoclastic figure, who being a woman exposed the demonic side of the religious fanatics.

> The mullahs who would murder me will kill everything progressive in Bangladesh if they are allowed to prevail. It is my duty to try to protect my beautiful country from them and I call on all those who share my values to help me defend my rights.
>
> (*Ibid.*, ix)

It has already been proved of the failure of the two nation theory on the political sphere. The book taken as a cult reveals the virus of communalism that has taken birth at the back of Bangladesh's liberation movements. I am referring the book as a 'cult', as it is first of its kind to bring out the gruesome picture of religious fanaticism.

The book focuses on how a Hindu family is crushed and destroyed for being a minority community in an Islamic state. The frequent question that can be raised while reading *Lajja* is that is Religion bigger than Humanism? And therefore the author dedicates the book to the people of Indian subcontinent, saying

> Let another name for Religion be Humanism.

Religion, an integral part of a community and culture is exploited and avenged upon in *Lajja to* show loyalty towards it.

The poignancy and irony of the situation is highlighted when Sudhamoy's family and many Hindu families had to pay the price of Babri Masjid killings in India. This concludes that language, norms, religion, tradition and habits shape an identity but at the time of crisis it might grapple an individual's existence.

> But why had they abducted Maya? Because she was Hindu?
>
> How much more rape, bloodshed, and loss of property were the Hindus going to suffer as the price for staying on in this country?
>
> (*Ibid.*, 152)

Sudhamoy's family lives in Bangladesh treating it to be their motherland and as it is supposed to be. To show allegiance and affirmation to the cultural community of Bangladesh and to identify with a common Islamic identity the family abandons many of its cultural signifiers.

> Kironmoyee had stopped using sindur in the parting in her hair and loha and sankha on her wrists as was expected of every married Hindu woman.... Sudhamoy, too, had given up his beloved dhuti.
>
> (*Ibid.*, 97)

The spirit of being a part of an Islamic country, does not restrict Sudhamoy from eating beef and,

> after a good deal of cajoling on Sudhamoy's part who had explained to his wife, at great length the futility and illogicality of observing such customs.
>
> (*Ibid.*, 64)

This could have been an effort by Sudhamoy to create space and identity for his family in a land which is dominated by Muslim subjects. He tries to negotiate with the world around him, keeping aside his own religious beliefs and values, to avoid political and religious persecution, and other inhospitable conditions for future.

The geographical division of the sub-continent along religious lines creates separate states for individual religious groups. In Bangladesh,

> by declaring Islam as the national religion, aren't the citizen of this country who are not Muslim deprived of the nation's support.
>
> (*Ibid.*, 87)

This explains the crust of the problem that has been issued through partition and continuous to loom large every time a crisis is precipitated, whenever a riot occurs, each time the question of the 'other' comes home with violence.

Sudhamoy's and the family's efforts at a complete assimilation and identification with Islamic culture and codes fail to protect them. The marginal religious status of Sudhamoy in Bangladesh, makes him go through three governing attitude that explains the meeting of two cultures—imitation, assimilation and rejection.

Maya is abducted and possibly raped Muslim extremists. This makes Sudhamoy and Suranjan notion of considering Bangladesh as their homeland is thwarted. Their attempt to synthesis with the precepts of Islamic community is met with violent rejection, due to the communal construction of the society. The author describes a society that is infested with gross discrimination and an authorial religious atmosphere. The book is an indictment on the secular nature of Bangladesh that it preaches.

> Democracy was clearly not strong enough to arrest the spread of communalism. On the other hand, the communal groups had much more strength and working towards the fulfillment of their goals.
>
> (*Ibid.*, 178)
>
> The façade of secularism, democracy, idealism is exposed by Nasrin, in the hope for a better future for both the communities, the Hindus and Muslims of Bangladesh.
>
> (Swain, 2000:137-39)

The study of the social and cultural background of the three nations—India, Pakistan and Bangladesh—propose that these countries share a common history and cultural memory which gives its populace a unique ethos—a blend of cultures and a variety of societies so well exemplified by the authors of the three nations respectively.

References

Beauvoir, Simone de: *The Second Sex*. UK; Random House; 1997.

Gandhi, Mahatma: *Hind Swaraj* or *Indian Home Rule* (1909). Ahmadabad; Navjivan Trust; 1938, 1996.

Jain, Jasbir: *Reading Partition/Living Partition*. New Delhi; Rawat Publication; 2007.

Kapur, Manju: *Difficult Daughters*. New Delhi; Faber and Faber; 1998.

Kapur, Manju: *A Married Woman*. New Delhi; India Ink (Roli Books); 2002.

Kapur, Manju: *Home*. New Delhi; Random House India; 2006.

Kapadia Novy, Dodiya Jaydipsinh and Dhawan R.K: Parsi Fiction. New Delhi; Prestige Books; 2001.

Moghissi, Haideh: *Feminism and Islamic Fundamentalism—The Limits of Postmodern Analysis*. Delhi; Oxford University Press, 1999.

Momen, Abul: Sampark, *Journal of Global Understanding*. Bangladesh Yesterday, Today and Tomorrow, January-March 1999.

Nasrin, Taslima: *Lajja*. New Delhi; Penguin Books; 1993.

Ramakrishna, E.V.: *Narrating India: The Novel in Search of Nation*. Delhi; Sahitya Akademy; 2005.

Sidhwa, Bapsi: *Ice-Candy-Man*. New Delhi; Penguin Books; 1988.

Sidhwa, Bapsi: *The Pakistani Bride*. New Delhi; Penguin Books; 1990.

Sidhwa, Bapsi: *The Crow Eaters*. New Delhi; Penguin Books; 1980.

Sidhwa, Bapsi: *An American Brat*. New Delhi; Penguin Books; 1994.

Swain, S.P.: *The Feminine Voice in Indian Fiction*. Delhi Asia Book Club; 2000.

Conclusion

> A nation is a soul, a spiritual principle...and among all its cults, that of the ancestors is the most legitimate, for the ancestors have made us what we are. A heroic past, great men, glory (by which I understand genuine glory), this is the social capital upon which one bases a national idea. More valuable...is the fact of sharing, in the past, a glorious heritage and regrets, and of having, in the future (a shared programme) to put into effect.
>
> (Bhabha, 1990:19)

> This idea of a common past, of shared sorrows and joys that connect the people, can also lend itself into wide interpretations and analysis. On June 3, 1947, a partition of the Indian sub-continent was announced and the historiography of the sub-continent hides itself into a charted silence, as 1947 marked the end of the most histories of the regions. With the attainment of nationalism and the solemnization of statehood, the studies of particular nation-states, branched out in the margins of newly created states of 'India', 'Pakistan' and 'Bangladesh'.
>
> (Bagchi and Dasgupta, 2003:4-10)

The 'Hindu', 'Muslim' and 'Bengali Muslims' discourses acts upon this shared identity, vis-à-vis, calls for interpretation of exclusive, individual identities. The bonds historical, cultural, linguistics and religion—are underlined to propose and imply the concept of nation, and national and therefore particular entities within each community. This calls for the 'otherness' that explains the essence and identity of each group. It is this backdrop that has been used by the three writers—Manju Kapur, Bapsi Sidhwa and Taslima Nasrin in their respective novels.

The studies posit the distinguished identities and self of each writer in reference to their approach in dealing with discourses of their nations. Manju Kapur, a representative writer of India, Sidhwa from Pakistan and Taslima Nasrin a Bengali Bangladeshi writer, in their texts present the 'ties', 'differences' and 'complexities' of Hindu, Muslim and Bengali Muslim identities and are exemplified in the novels chosen for study.

> The study of the three nations through the eyes of the three writers brings out the contrasts and similarities in the contending identities of the members of their respective communities. The study of the texts posits the crisis that emerged out, at the dawn of the new-nation states in 1947, with a deep anxiety to learn about the future of secular nation states.
>
> (Singh, 1997:45-50)

The women writers of the three nations bring out their involvement with feminist modulations and their social and literary pertinence. Marginalization of subjects and themes which could be of major consequence for women's community, as a whole has been dealt with. This gives a major significance to female relations in respect to the community they belong to.

Manju Kapur, Bapsi Sidhwa and Taslima Nasrin have made an intellectual effort to analyze the various dimensions of feminism and have identified feminine subjection as a social disease caused by patriarchal, class based and economic factors.

Bibliography

Bagchi, Jasodhara and Dasgupta, Subhoranjan. *The Trauma and Triumph of Gender and Partition.* New Delhi; Shree Publication; 2003.

Batulia, Urvashi. *The Other Side of Silence, Voices from the Partition of India.* New Delhi; Penguin; 1998.

Beauvoir, Simone de. *The Second Sex.* UK; Random House; 1997.

Bhabha, Homi K. (ed). *Nation and Narration.* USA; Routledge; 1990.

Bhasin, Kamala. *Understanding Gender.* New Delhi; Kali for Women; 2000.

Eichenbaum, *Luise and Susie Orbach. Understanding Women.* England; Penguin Books; 1992.

Gandhi, Mahatma. *Hind Swaraj or Indian Home Rule* (1909). Ahmadabad; Navjivan Trust; 1938, 1996.

Jain, Jasbir. *Reading Partition/Living Partition.* New Delhi, Rawat Publication; 2007.

Kapadia, Novy and Dodiya, Jaydipsinh and Dhawan, R.K. *Parsi Fiction.* New Delhi; Prestige Books; 2001.

Kapur, Manju. *A Married Woman.* New Delhi; India Ink (Roli Books); 2002.

Kapur, Manju. *Difficult Daughters.* New Delhi; Faber and Faber, 1998.

Kapur, Manju. *Home.* New Delhi; Random House India; 2006.

Kiberd, Declan. *Men and Feminism in Modern Literature*. Delhi; Macmillan Press; 1985.

Manto, Saadat Hasan. *Toba Tek Singh*, translated from Urdu by Frances W. Pritchett, 1955.

Moghissi, Haideh. *Feminism and Islamic Fundamentalism—The Limits of Postmodern Analysis*. Delhi; Oxford University Press, 1999.

Momen, Abul. *Sampark, Journal of Global Understanding. Bangladesh Yesterday, Today and Tomorrow*, January-March; 1999.

Myles, Anita. *Feminism and the Post-Modern India*. Delhi Sarup & Sons, 2006.

Nasrin, Taslima. *Lajja*. New Delhi; Penguin Books; 1993.

Ramakrishna, E.V. *Narrating India. The Novel in Search of Nation*. Delhi; Sahitya Akademy; 2005.

Sidhwa, Bapsi. *An American Brat*. New Delhi; Penguin Books; 1994.

Sidhwa, Bapsi. *Ice-Candy-Man*. New Delhi; Penguin Books; 1988.

Sidhwa, Bapsi. *Points of Departure: International Writers on Writing and Politics*. 1989.

Sidhwa, Bapsi. *The Crow Eaters*. New Delhi; Penguin Books; 1980.

Sidhwa, Bapsi. *The Pakistani Bride*. New Delhi; Penguin Books; 1990.

Singh, Charu Sheel. *Women about Women in Indian Literature in English*. New Delhi; Anmol Publication; 1998.

Singh, Jyoti. *Indian Women Novelists*. Delhi; Rawat Publication; 2007.

Singh, Kushwant (translator). *Punjabi Poems of Amrita Pritam*. New Delhi; 2009.

Singh, R.A. *Post Colonial Indian English Writing*. New Delhi; Bihari Publication; 1997.

Swain, S.P. *The Feminine Voice in Indian Fiction*, Delhi; Asia Book Club; 2000.

Interview:

Dalmia, Yashodhara "An Interview with Anita Desai", *The Times of India*, 29th April, 1979.

Article: 'Oxford Journals'

'Sidhwa Bapsi and Butulia Urvashi: '*Discuss the Partition of India Subcontinent*'; OUP (2000), New Delhi.

Article: Desai Anita:

"*Woman Writers*", Quest No. 65, April-June 1970.